Love Your Woman

*Releasing the mystery, grace,
and passion in your mate.*

By Douglas Michael Bankson

TABLE OF CONTENTS

INTRODUCTION

How can a man love his woman? What is a woman's definition of love? Surely there aren't enough trees in the forest to make enough pages to fill enough books to answer that one. It is as complex as there are women on the earth. But there are some basics that you need to know to help you in your quest.

My purpose in this writing is to have a book that "Every wife wishes her husband would read," while having something enjoyable enough that every man actually will. I endeavor to capture the essence of what a woman really longs for in her husband, and to put it in a practical way that every man can understand and follow through. My goal is not only to see marriages rescued from mediocrity, frustration, and dissolution, but also enhanced to a level of mutual joy and fulfillment. From the "I Do's" to the "Ooh la la's," let's enjoy the journey together as we unlock secrets to marital joy and bliss.

If you have been married for any length of time, I'm sure you've found the old adage true, "Happy wife, happy life." But is it really possible to have a happy wife? Is it possible to understand your wife and meet her needs? Absolutely! God gives you the blueprint, and by following His design, you can learn how to really love your woman.

Douglas M. Bankson

DEDICATION

To my beloved bride, Jeri Lynn Bankson

Honey,

What an amazing journey we have had so far. It seems like just yesterday we were having that strawberry pie fight at your parent's house, and here we are so many years later, more in love than the day we first met. You are such a wonderful woman, wife, and mother, and I never would have written this book if it weren't for you. You captivate me in a way no one else can, and have a place in my heart that no one else ever will. I love your funny little ways and I'm mesmerized by your beauty every time you walk by. You are the greatest blessing the Lord has given me in this life, and I credit the success of our relationship to you. You are a Christ-like example and you are loved and admired by all who know you. You are my bride, my companion, my lover, and my best friend. To me, there could be no one else to whom I could dedicate this book, and so I do to you, with all my heart and devotion.

Forever,

Doug

P.S. How about another strawberry pie fight? I'll bring the whipped cream!!

ACKNOWLEDGEMENTS

There are so many influences throughout a lifetime who make you who you are, and there is no way to acknowledge all who have played a part, but here are a few who have labored on this project:

Pastor Jeri Bankson - I thought writing was the hard part, but your oversight in editing brought out the full dimension of this book that was intended. Thank you once again honey for all you have done! You are my one and only, and I couldn't do it without you, and wouldn't want to!

Pastor Vicki Mock - What can I say? You're an amazing person and such a gift of God to my wife and me. You're the most versatile person we know, and always with a fun sense of humor that lightens the load. We're so blessed to have you as part of our team, and your tireless hours of helping my wife during editing are invaluable. Thank you for all you and your husband Coby do for Jesus, and for us.

Pastor Benjamin Bankson - Although you are our firstborn, you were loaned to us from God and are a great strength and help in the ministry. Your creative talents astound me, and your diligence blesses me. I am proud to call you my son, and blessed to serve the Lord together.

Michael Cairnes - You, my friend, not only have a gift from God, you *are* a gift from God. We enjoy your professionalism in photography, and you have a way of bringing out the joy in others. Thank you for making us look so good!

FOREWORD

In a day when pastors are being absolutely dismayed and amazed that some of the strongest marriages in their congregations, the solid citizens that have for years held their ministries up in prayers and in finance, are suddenly coming to them with the startling news that their marriages are over... she has had an affair going for years...he didn't mean to but he has fallen in love with his business associate...saying things like "the children are going to be alright; they're flexible while they're young" "I have prayed and I know this is alright with God...He told me so while I was praying," Pastor Doug Bankson has found a way to get the attention, particularly of the male of the species.

His book is filled with humor that draws very powerful conclusions. His insight into the **man problem** that affects marriages is done in an attention-keeping manner even for the most hopeless of masculine messes among us.

This book is scripturally accurate and filled with revelation that will bless any man who reads it with an open mind and a heart to become what God wants him to be as a husband and father. It is particularly needful in a day when, in the church, one out of two marriages end in divorce. This causes devastation of the children involved, who are shattered because mom and dad suddenly are no longer there as a unit.

For more than thirty years of relationship, I have known Doug Bankson to be a strong man of God with a family that is stellar in makeup and Christian character. I highly recommend this book to men who are married, or ever hope to be.

Blessing is to be found in these pages...

Pastor Larry Gordon
Founder/Senior Pastor, Cornerstone World Outreach

I just completed reading the manuscript for Pastor Doug Bankson's book; Love Your Woman. I found it to be very refreshing and insightful. It covers this important subject scripturally, intellectually and most of all in a non-religious way that everyone can relate to.

The book is practical and if you follow the principles, you will not only have a wonderful marriage, but you will spice up your love life with the wife of your youth. Learn to listen to and communicate with your wife, and you (with God's help) will overcome every obstacle that may come your way.

I highly recommend this book. If you are married it will help you keep the flame burning. If you are single, it gives you good insight and instruction for the day that you will find that good thing and obtain favor with the Lord.

Dr. Michael Landsman, Ph.D; Ed.D.
Assistant Dean Rhema Training Center
Rhema Bible Church South Africa

This book, *Love Your Woman,* is extremely and urgently needed in the body of Christ today. The divorce and separation rate, even among God's people, is unacceptable. I appreciate Pastor Bankson for taking the time to address these issues. There are things in this book that no one seems to want to deal with. The book is easy reading and very inspiring. It is absolutely life-changing, and it is obvious that much prayer went into it. You can feel the anointing come upon you as you read each page.

My Vickie and I courted for five years and have been married for forty. We raised our children in the gospel, and we are now helping with our seven grandchildren. We have been together forty-five years and have enjoyed what many call a storybook marriage. Many of the secrets revealed in this book are the very principles of life that have enriched our life as a couple.

Since meeting Jesus, I have recognized the anointing on my life to "husband." I believe the word "husband" is a synonym for "anointing," just like the word "wife" is a synonym for the word "anointing." You can always tell when a man is being "wifed" biblically by a Proverbs 31 virtuous woman (which means an anointed woman). The Holy Spirit is upon her to relieve the burden and destroy the yoke of the world, the flesh, and satan that try to get upon her man, her household, and her children.

The same is true with a married woman who has been "husbanded" properly by her man. He should also be flowing in the virtues of the great Holy Spirit. He brings great release to his wife and causes her to be free from the yoke of satan and the burden of this life. You could say he is a "virtuous man," anointed by God to fulfill the call of God on his life. Vickie and I have always said that if you can be a Christian at home and have the fruit of the Spirit operating in your marriage at home, you will always live a happy life.

I have watched Pastor Doug through the years and how he loves his bride, cherishes her, and treats her with respect, yet still leads her and is responsible before God as her husband. The absolute beauty of this book is that it's written by a man who has walked out these things. It is far beyond theory and suggestion; it is proven. Thank you, Doug, for not only a great writing but for living and practicing what you preach. I salute you for writing this book, and I also salute your lifestyle and your many years of walking out the things you have now so beautifully put on the printed page. I wish every man and woman could read this book; for it would surely anoint them in their marriage and in their bedroom and enable them to live a much higher quality of life. Job well done!

Dr. Mark T. Barclay
Founder/ Senior Pastor, Living Word Church
President, Mark T. Barclay Ministries

I have been married to my husband Mark Barclay for 40 years. This writing of Pastor Doug's is tremendous. We admire the fact that Doug and Jeri live and practice what they preach. This book is an expression of the beautiful life they live together. Every man and woman should read it and perhaps read it together.

Vickie Barclay

CHAPTER 1

WHAT'S LOVE GOT TO DO WITH IT?

W hat's love got to do with it? To the woman the answer is simple: *everything*.

But for us as men, understanding that need seems anything but simple.

Men are fixers by nature. We want to solve problems. It is in our make up; it's what we *do*. We are designed by God to protect, preserve, and defend. We will fight for our woman, provide for our woman, build her a home, fix her car, mow the lawn, kill bugs... but *love* her?

For all of our problem-solving prowess, we have one big problem: we don't know what love means! What is a woman's definition of love? As men we want to buy love, give love, and of course, make love. But what does it really mean to love a woman?

I can only imagine the day Adam first saw Eve; sunshine, free food, and now a beautiful, naked woman! Life was complete! Adam was set, or so it seemed. What he didn't realize is that as a problem solver, God had just given him the ultimate Rubik's Cube®. It wasn't meant to bring frustration, but to be the ultimate quest, the ultimate riddle, the ultimate conquest. That's right; she was the Ulti-Mate! He would spend the rest of eternity pursuing, discovering, and enjoying this mystery called woman.

But really, God had just given Adam a key: the key to understanding God Himself. The Bible says that God is love. In giving him a woman, God had just given him the ability to discover the true meaning of love. The adventure from attraction to courtship to marriage is designed to teach us the true nature of love; both its pursuit and fulfillment.

So let us go bravely, men. Let us press onward if we dare. Let us boldly go where no man has gone before! Into the mind of a woman!!

CHAPTER 2

LOVE IS LIKE
A BOOMERANG!

Are you still with me? Good! Then you passed the first test! The fact that you are reading has already earned you brownie points with your wife. That is the purpose, right? To make her happy so you can make love...tonight! Right?

I'll never forget the week before I was to get married. Two men in our church who had been married for some time stopped me in the hallway to give me some friendly advice. Their advice was this: Do and say whatever she wants, and always agree with her, or you won't "get any." I'm sure they thought they were helping me out, but their advice seemed extremely shallow and self-serving. (Incidentally, both of their marriages ended in divorce... I wonder why. Hmmm.)

Their definition of love was the world's definition of love. To the worldly way of thinking, the object is always self. It is about how it makes *me* feel, and whether *I'm* fulfilled. Even the famous Jerry McGuire line, "You complete me" is still about...well...*ME*. The real key to love is not about being the receiver, but being the giver. It is in this dimension that we find the wonderful secret about love: love is like a boomerang! The more you give, the more it comes back to you. And there is real truth to what Jesus Himself said:

"...It is more blessed to give than to receive."
Acts 20:35b KJV

God's kind of love is the best. He is our designer, architect, and manufacturer. He knows how to get top performance out of His creation. That's got to speak to us men. We are all about making it bigger, faster, stronger. (We're not talking "Smilin' Bob" here. Hint: Viagra®.) God didn't create us with great potential only to put a limiter on us. He wants us to get the best out of life! The problem is that we men don't like reading directions. We approach love from the "hands on" method. We try to figure it out as we go. We make mistakes, mess things up, and take wrong turns, only to be too proud to ask for directions.

So What is God's Definition of Love?

God is love. Everything about Him is love. All of His motives for everything He does are out of love. So let's take a look at His model for love.

Love Always Gives

God so loved the world that He gave. It is the truest expression of love. This is one of the basic needs of mankind. What is the point of having things if you can't share them? When you love, you want to share all you have with the one you love. God was not content to merely own all things. He created the whole world for the express purpose of giving it to us, and sharing it with us. And when man sinned, God gave the ultimate gift; His own son to purchase us. Love spares no expense! Love gives!!

LOVE MUST HAVE A TARGET

It's impossible to give without a receiver. Therefore the object of love is the one that is receiving. The whole focus is the fulfillment of the beneficiary of that love. Love's fulfillment is the joy of the recipient. This is what Jesus meant by, "It's more blessed to give than to receive."

Their happiness brings you happiness. Yet with all His giving, God is never empty, but always fulfilled and happy. It is because this is the nature of love. The more you give; the more joy and fulfillment you get.

LOVE IS LIKE OXYGEN

There really was truth to that song. We are wired with the need to both give and receive love. We need a steady stream of inhaling and exhaling or we will pass out. Love is meant to be shared. It is like a pass in football, it's incomplete without a receiver catching the pass. But nothing is sweeter than a QB and WR connecting for a TD! (I thought a little football analogy might help keep your attention, especially for you that are just looking to score.) And lest you think this book is about shaming you for wanting to have sex, hold on to your shorts. We'll get to that. It is, after all, God's idea and His wedding gift. (By the way, a woman wants to be fulfilled in the bedroom too.)

Love is the Goal

Just as every sport has a goal line, a home base, a basket, a target; so love needs to be the goal. The Apostle Paul taught Timothy that love should be our aim.

> *"But the goal of our instruction is love from a pure heart and a good conscience and a sincere faith."*
> *I Timothy 1:5 NASV*

Apply this to your marriage and your wife; let loving her be your aim. Let it be your goal. Win her heart! Fulfill her dreams! Be the world's greatest lover!! Wilt Chamberlain boasted he had slept with over 1,000 women, but just like King Solomon he was still unfulfilled. It's because when you live to fulfill yourself, you end up empty; but when you live to give, you never run out. Sex is not the goal; love is the goal. Sex is a bi-product, and one important expression of love. If you will aim at love, you will end up getting what all the other men want. Like Jesus said:

> *"But seek first the Kingdom of God and His righ-*
> *teousness, and all these things* (that the world seeks)
> *shall be added to you."*
> *Matthew 6:33 NKJV*

There was once a poll taken about who were the most sexually gratified. It was a broad-based poll with Christian and non-Christian respondents alike, and by married and non-married alike. The interesting thing is that the most sexually satisfied group that took the poll was spirit-filled Christians! I believe when we follow God's principles in our life to love first, all the blessings become a natural progression.

God's love is unconditional. It is a pure example of the way we are to love. Like the old hymn says:

"He loved me ere I knew Him;
Now all my love is due Him." [1]

When you sow love, you will reap love; and the kind of love you sow is the kind you will reap. If your love is conditional, then you may end up getting that kind back. But when you love like God does, that is what you will reap.

I must say at this point that the true secret to happiness begins by a right and good relationship with God. No mate can fill the void that God is meant to fill. Without His unconditional love it is hard, if not impossible, to be happy in life.

So what are the keys to loving your woman? Let's discuss a few.

LOVE IS A CHOICE

"I command you to be in love!" Sounds ridiculous, and of course that is not what God says to us. He has given us a free will and thanks to that "replenish the earth" thing, there are a lot of fish in the sea. But once we have played the dating game and have finally found that special someone, the responsibility to love her is not an option. We are commanded to love them.

"Husbands, love your wives..."
Ephesians 5:24a KJV

Looks so simple doesn't it? Four little words. Oh, but it can take a lifetime to figure them out.

So let's get back to that command.

The fact that God commands us to **love our wives** tells us something important. Love is a choice. A command is something you can choose to obey, whether you feel like it or not. It is not an emotion, although it can produce great emotion. It is not something you can fall in and out of; although attraction can encourage us to want to make that choice. It is not goose bumps, although they can be the reward of making that choice. It is a choice that we can make.

God would never tell us to do something that is impossible to do, because that would be entirely unjust and we know that God is just. In fact, God proved that love is a choice. He loved us before we loved Him; while we were yet sinners (in rebellion against Him) He loved us, and sent His Son to die for us. No matter how much we screw things up, He is always ready to forgive us and draw us back in.

"Husbands, love your wives."

She is not like a set of golf clubs that we use until the next model comes along. She is not something we get tired of and lose interest in. She is not some*thing* at all. She is some*one*.

Actually, love was never meant for things. We can enjoy things. I enjoy my Harley-Davidson VROD, 2003 100th anniversary edition, silver and black with gold pinstripes and winged tank emblem, 1143 screaming cc's, with lowered suspension, chrome upgrade kit, sport seat, solid aluminum wheels, hollowed baffles, "I can show you pictures if you like" motorcycle. But I love my wife, who's favorite color is...um...she loves to eat at...um...our anniversary is...um...yeah...I love my wife. You get what I'm saying?

Again, there's nothing wrong with **enjoying things**:

> *"...God who gives us richly <u>all things to enjoy</u>."*
> *I Timothy 6:17 NKJV*

But love is reserved for people; first God, and then our wife. Period. No one and nothing should come before them.

So are we banished to a life of emotionless servitude of marital duty? Absolutely not! Once the choice to love is made, a wonderful thing happens; the choice to love gives birth to the emotions of love!

I will be open here. In our, as of this writing, 23 years of wedded bliss, I have had opportunities for love to grow cold and stale. I have had times to be upset and irritated with my wife. (Of course it's always my fault — she is proofreading this you know.)

Seriously, I remember one time being in my garage and being really irritated at her. I don't even know what it was about, but I was angry at something, and I could feel the walls of resentment beginning to grow inside me. That's when I applied this principle. I turned that anger toward the devil and told him emphatically, "No! I love my wife!! You will NOT build a wall of resentment in me!" I then asked the Lord to forgive me for my resentments, and began to pray for her and say over and over again, "I love my wife, I love my wife, I LOVE MY WIFE!" As I did, a transformation began to happen and the emotions of love filled me up. It took just a few minutes, but by the time I was done, I walked into the house and there she was in the kitchen. I walked up behind her and put my arms around her and told her how much I loved her. She responded the same way, and we were like two newlyweds!

Now if you let that wall of resentment build it may take a little longer, but the fact remains: the choice to love gives birth to the emotions of love. I dare you to try it right now. Put this book down, stir your heart, and then go tell your wife that you love her.

WHAT DO YOU MEAN, IT'S MY FAULT?

"You'll reap what you sow!!" This phrase conjures up an image of a wrinkled old lady with a long bony finger pointing down as she looks over the top of her wire rims, with the secret desire for you to get what's coming to you. The truth is that discovering this powerful law of reciprocity is one of the keys to a happy and healthy life, not to mention marriage.

Marriage, some have said, is a 50/50 proposition. Not so. It is a 100/100, "all in" kind of relationship. If you live 50/50, all it takes is one of you to perceive that the other is only giving 49%, and the battle begins. Remember this, YOU CAN'T CHANGE YOUR WIFE! (Oh, you figured that out already.) Only God can. The only thing you can control is what you sow. And God is the Lord of your harvest!

If you will sow in love, you can expect to receive the same… eventually. You see, a wise farmer knows if he sows today, it takes time for that seed to grow, but if he will cultivate, water, weed, and protect it, it will reap a multiplied harvest. In fact, the marriage you have today is the result of seeds you have sown in the past.

In my experience I have found that it takes a good five years for a marriage to become established. It's like a fruit tree. It takes awhile for the roots to grow strong and the tree to become acclimated to new soil. The shock of replanting is overcome, and the level of care and nutrients now has taken effect, whether good or bad. A tree can overcome a bad start with good care, and a tree with a good start can wilt if not kept with the same level of nutrition.

A marriage is the same way. After the initial five years or so, what you are reaping is more due to what you have sown than how your wife grew up. (It can take longer for those who get remarried after going through a divorce, due to the damage that can cause.) But no matter how rough a start you have, love conquers all. Love gives it time! Your greatest accomplishment is your wife, and it says the most about who you are.

So what can you do to make your marriage strong? How can you make sure the soil is full of nutrients so that there are years of sweet fruit instead of sour grapes? Here are a few ideas:

- Keep the tank full
- Put the lid down
- Water her with your words
- Tell her you love her
- Help without being asked
- Step away from the remote
- Romance her

Love is also demonstrated in our actions. Jesus demonstrated His love by laying down His life for us, and if He did that then surely we can lay down our lives for our wife.

Recently I had a real opportunity to demonstrate this very point. In all our 23 years of marriage I had somehow avoided the unpleasant task of purchasing, shall we say, certain products that are reserved for the feminine gender. One day I made the unfortunate mistake of calling home from town and asking if there was anything that I needed to pick up at the store. I was instructed that it was that "special time" and then given the brand names of what I was to acquire. I asked if there was anything else, *anything else* that I could get to make the purchase less obvious. Nothing. "OK. I can do this."

I walked sheepishly into the store and picked up a basket, and found my way to the feminine products. As I stood in the aisle looking at the wall of different items, my eyes began to blur and I wished I were in a more familiar setting such as automotive or electronics. Nearby was a lady shopper, and I tried to avoid contact, but she took a step toward me, paused for a second, looked up and smiled and said, "You're a good man."

I told her it had been a tough week, and she helped me find the correct make and model, and I was off to the register. As I walked, it began to sink in; "You're a good man." I figured if Christ could die on a cross, I could surely die of embarrassment. I decided I would add some flowers (three bundles for $10) and walked to the cashier, where I mumbled something that seemed much more clever in my head than in my mouth. As I walked to the car, I felt like a hero, and that's how I was greeted at home.

So love needs to be demonstrated in such a way that it lays down its life for the one who is loved, and what you put into your marriage is what you will get out of it.

CHAPTER 3

WHO'S THE BOSS?

"**G**overnment is evil!" So seems to be the modern cry, in an era where more and more of our take home pay isn't taken home. But is that the answer? Is government evil? The answer is NO. Government is not evil; EVIL government is evil. Overreaching government is evil. Intrusive government is evil. But government in its right place is good and beneficial to everyone concerned. Authority is a good thing when it is there to protect and preserve our liberties. So it is with headship in a marriage.

In this politically correct, overcharged world we live in, it is almost taboo to discuss headship and authority when it comes to marriage. For that matter, marriage itself is under attack as antiquated. We see the confusion of the sexes as men are routinely "feminized," and women are "masculinized." Mankind is fighting the norms and thus abnormality is becoming the norm to many. The problem is that we are wired by God from birth, and no amount of gender modification on any level can truly fulfill the answer to the question, "Who am I?" It is in God's order that we find true fulfillment, and there is a godly order for marriage to be truly fulfilling.

So who *is* the boss? Are men better than women or vice-versa? First of all, it is important to note that in Christ there is neither male nor female. There is also a difference between men and women roles inside vs. outside of marriage. In fact, many have misinterpreted whole passages of scripture because they wrongly interpreted the difference between "women" and "men" as plural, vs. "the woman" and "the man" as singular. Men are not over women, neither are women over men, but a married woman needs to respect the positional authority that God has given her husband, and a husband must not abuse that authority either.

Within the covenant of marriage there must be an order for things to flow correctly. For example, two people may be neighbors. They have no authority over one another, just the responsibility to govern their personal lives and be good neighbors. Now let's say that they both work for the same company, but one is the boss. In the work environment there is now an order and you have authority and submission that come into play. It would be wrong for the boss to "overlord" their authority, and it would also be wrong for the subordinate worker to undermine or usurp that same authority. For some reason we can all see that this is not only right but a good and profitable way to conduct business, and yet when it comes to the home, we fight this model. Yet even this is not the best understanding of the husband/wife relationship. (This would actually better describe a parent/child relationship.)

Now let's take it a step further. Let's say that both neighbors are in upper management, and yet one is in a more senior role. They are a team, each with responsibilities and authority, working together for the good of the company and the benefit of the employees. They recognize not only the position each has, but also the authority structure. This is a different dynamic than the "employer/employee" model. This is rather a collaboration of two management level employees on an intellectually equal field, one being the CEO (chief executive officer) and the other being the COO (chief operating officer). Decisions are not made unilaterally, but rather with both minds and all talents working together.

The CEO must make the call and therefore must have the final word, but he is not a tyrant wielding bombastic authority. He should not be demeaning to the COO! It would be an ignorant leader who would not gather intelligence before making decisions. Imagine the CEO treating the COO like an underling; merely barking out orders; angry if nothing gets done to their liking. I say he will have a very discouraged and angry COO who will eventually not want to stay with the company!

Unfortunately, too many men have done this until their wife has been broken, and then when the wife leaves, they blame her. All the while it was their poor leadership that did not recognize and value their wife until it was too late. The bottom line is that your wife is not your employee, but your equal who submits to your positional authority, and if handled correctly will do so out of respect earned rather than respect demanded.

The Bible says in Ecclesiastes that two are better than one. Two perspectives can bring greater depth perception and help make better decisions. If you don't believe this, try driving while covering one eye. Both can do the job alone, but together there is a better picture. Isn't it interesting that God gave us two eyes and yet one is dominant? When the hands fold, one thumb is above the other, but both opposable thumbs were God's idea. You see God created man, both male and female. He **called** *their* **name Adam**, which interpreted means mankind.

"Male and female created he them; and blessed them, and <u>called their name Adam</u>, in the day when they were created."

Genesis 5:2 KJV

We were meant by God to be a team together, two eyes to see the same picture from slightly different angles, not fighting for position but working together. We don't want to be "crossed," since that would only lead to double vision!

This is the best picture of the home as God designed it to function, and it is a great model! In fact, it is the best model for a safe, healthy, and prosperous family.

When Adam and Eve were created, God made them senior management of planet earth. He gave them authority over all His creation and the ability to make "little employees." And there's a great benefit package: **He blessed them**!

"And <u>God blessed them</u>, and God said unto them, be fruitful and multiply, and replenish the earth, and subdue it: and have dominion…"

Genesis 1:28a KJV

Notice it says He blessed *them*. This is important to note. The blessing in a marriage can only be accessed in unity together. It is like the launch keys for a nuclear missile! They must both be present and turned in unison to unleash the power!

LEADING WITH LOVE

One of the favorite, oft quoted scriptures most married men know by heart is:

> *"Wives submit yourselves unto your own husbands*
> *as unto the Lord; For the <u>husband is the head of</u>*
> *<u>the wife</u> even as <u>Christ is the head of the church</u>..."*
> *Ephesians 5:22-23a KJV*

While this is absolutely true, this is only a partial statement, and misleading without the rest of the statement and context. Let me also give you a little friendly advice; verse 22 was written mainly to the wife to tell her how to respond to your leadership (remember the corporate team concept). You would do well to ask the Holy Spirit to deal with her if you feel she's not living up to her end of the bargain, and start with verse 23 and focus on your job. How would you like it if a team partner was always looking over your shoulder to make sure you do your work?

You may say, "That's the problem; I am trying to be the **head** and she won't let me." Yes, there are times that some wives try to usurp the authority, but there is a right way and a wrong way to deal with this. The answer is found as you continue reading the passage. So many times we start with the first phrase and forget the rest. We see it as an ultimate authority, a dominating lordship. "After all, Sarah called Abraham Lord!" (Yes, master.) You may reason, "**Christ is the head of the church** and we have that same level of authority over our wives," but the real balance is found in the rest of the verse:

> *"...and He is the <u>Savior</u> of the body."*
> *Ephesians 5:23b KJV*

This means that your authority starts with leading them to Christ! And you do this by example not by demand! Did He demand you to get saved, or didn't He rather patiently draw your heart until you heard His?

It goes on to say in verse 25:

> ***"Husbands, love your wives, <u>as Christ loved the</u> <u>church</u>..."***
>
> *Ephesians 5:25a KJV*

Before you judge her for not submitting, ask yourself if you are loving her **as Christ loved the church**. The biggest word in this phrase is, "AS." Now let me ask you, did Christ start loving you before or after you straightened up? Is He patient with you even when you don't obey Him? Do I need to go on? You can fill in the blanks. We want the lordship and absolute obedience from our wives coupled with unwavering respect, but we have the greater responsibility to love and lead whether she does her part or not. This takes a real man! That is the "laying down your life" kind of love He was talking about.

> ***"...<u>and gave Himself</u> for it."***
>
> *Ephesians 5:25b KJV*

Notice it says here, **"and gave Himself."** This is absolutely key! Yes, your wife wants you to take good care of her, but what she really wants is YOU! It is easier for us to turn over the paycheck and crawl into our man caves at the end of the day with a remote in one hand and a beverage in the other believing we've done our part, than it is to open up and share our hearts and dreams.

I'm not talking about wearing a doily and being prissy; I'm talking about friendship and companionship. As a husband, it is your responsibility to make sure she is fulfilled as a person with her own desires and dreams. She didn't marry you so she would have someone else to cook for, clean up after, and service whenever you feel like it! She's not a slave! She's not a robot! She's your wife! And by the way, she's God's daughter. (Just in case there are any ladies reading and underlining this for your husband, he also didn't marry you just to have someone to nag him for all his faults, and play "Mother-May-I" when he misses step #9 on the "10 things you must do to get sex" list.)

Jesus actually said the main reason divorce was allowed under Moses' law was because of the hardness of people's hearts. Basically, because we are stubborn hard-hearted, proud, and childish. So man-up, woman-up, GROW up! (That's what most pastors would like to say in a lot of marriage counseling sessions...session over.) Really folks love is better than that!

> *"Love is patient and is kind; love doesn't envy. Love doesn't brag, is not proud, doesn't behave itself inappropriately, doesn't seek its own way, is not provoked, takes no account of evil; doesn't rejoice in unrighteousness, but rejoices with the truth; bears all things, believes all things, hopes all things, endures all things. Love never fails. ... When I was a child, I spoke as a child, I felt as a child, I thought as a child. Now that I have become a man, I have put away childish things."*
> **I Corinthians 13:4-8, 11 WEB**

This may be especially difficult if you were raised in a military family or have a military background. We would love to have the "because I said so, that's why" kind of commanded respect because it is much easier than earning that respect. In times of danger or emergency you can demand that level based upon your authority, I would agree. But when it comes to your wife, there is a whole different dimension at play. (You will understand this more when we get to our chapter about the differences between men and women, but for now you'll just have to trust me on this one.)

Suffice to say, you did not marry a plebe, grunt, or gunny, you married your wife! I know, there are women in the military, but when it comes to home, leave the G.I. Joe/Jane thing on the battlefield; unless you want your home to become one! If you must have a military mindset, it's more like the concept of a wingman — together on a mission.

Whatever your background, you are in a leadership team now. You may be given a senior position, but she is also an officer who comes with authority. She must be respected as well, by the way. The Bible says that husbands must:

> *"…Giving <u>honor</u> to the wife, as to the <u>weaker vessel</u>… that your prayers may not be hindered."*
> *I Peter 3:7 NKJV*

So when you don't **honor** your wife, God will not **honor** you!! How about a little self-test? Take a look back on just this week alone and ask yourself how you've treated your wife. Would you want God, who is your superior and both you and your wife's Commander-in-Chief, to treat you in the same manner as you have treated her? Do you want God to ignore your desires, blow off your thoughts, or put off the things you need done?

You need to treat her as an intellectual equal who is equipped with vital information for all the decisions you must make… and all of your decisions ought to be predicated by that which makes her life easier. And that **weaker vessel** part, let's just say you should be glad she is not built like "Bruno" (more on that later as well).

So men, it is our responsibility to lead with love, just like Christ. And as the apostle John added, let us not love in word (only) but in deed and in truth.

CHAPTER 4

WHAT'S MY
JOB DESCRIPTION?

E very job should come with a job description, and being the head of the house is no different. Many of us just wing it based upon our interpretation or perhaps the only example we have had, our natural fathers. But generational and societal influences can sometimes alter and effect how we perceive our job as the head. Just as in a military scenario, a wrong mindset might have much to do with the frustration, lack of cooperation, and disillusionment that can set in on our marriages. So let's define our position as the "Head of the House," (i.e. "King of the Castle," "Master of our Domain," etc., etc.).

First, let's start with the phrase "Head of the House." This is actually a misnomer. The Bible does not say that we are the head of the house, but that we are **the head of the woman**.

> *"But I would have you know, that the head of every man is Christ; and <u>the head of the woman is the man</u>; and the head of Christ is God."*
> *I Corinthians 11:3 KJV*

In fact, the Bible says:

> *"I will therefore that the younger women marry, bear children, <u>guide the house</u>, give none occasion to the adversary to speak reproachfully."*
>
> *I Timothy 5:14 KJV*

She is to **guide the house** which comes from the Greek word *oikodespoteo* and means to be the head of the house, or quite literally, that she is the absolute ruler (despot) of the house. This is an interesting mix of the function of authority. It means that though you have an oversight authority, she has a functional authority in the home, which means when she says pick up your dirty underwear off the floor, you are supposed to obey her!

It's like at work, when you are asked to do a job, you are given the authority to do that job. A good leader (husband) will not frustrate his own management (wife), but will set the example to the employees (kids) by following the guidelines of the manager he hires. Of course he has the right to change things up, but if he's smart he won't micromanage.

So again, our position is to be **the head of the woman,** or **the wife** as it says in Ephesians:

> *"For the husband is the <u>head of the wife</u>, as also Christ is head of the church; and He is the <u>Savior of the body</u>."*
>
> *Ephesians 5:23 NKJV*

Our position and responsibilities can handily be summed up in four words: *Protection, Direction, Provision,* and *Leadership.*

PROTECTION

Notice in the verse just stated, the emphasis of what the head does. He is the **savior of the body.** In this passage the word **savior** comes from the Greek word *sozo,* which means *to save, deliver, or protect.* This is the number one job of the head. All that you do should be to protect your wife. Because we are three part beings, that means more than just physically protecting her from danger. We are spirit, soul, and body creatures, therefore our responsibility lies in all three areas.

We like to lead many times when it comes to the natural areas, but our first responsibility is to protect spiritually. We should not be the ones who have to be nagged into going to church, or praying together. We should be leading the way. Joshua (whose name incidentally means "savior" in Hebrew) made the classic statement:

> *"...As for me and my house, we will serve the Lord."*
> *Joshua 24:15b KJV*

This will give your wife a sense of stability. There's actually only one person that can make you treat your wife right: GOD. When He becomes the Lord of your life, the Holy Spirit can both guide you into all truth, and convict you when you are missing the mark. I know this is different if your wife is unsaved, and you will have to love her into the kingdom of God, but to those who already believe, they really want you to lead the way.

Take the initiative, but know this: you do not take Jesus' place over them any more than a pastor takes Jesus' place over you. You are His representative with authority, but she must choose to yield to that authority. You cannot lord it over her, or force your conscience over her. You must lead her with a loving hand.

Jesus is her Lord too. If your wife will not listen, chances are it is because you have created a callous upon her heart through your roughness.

Yes, there are those who try to usurp authority, but that is what my wife deals with in her book to them. We are working on ourselves in this book. No matter how callous your wife may be, if you will start turning that around by respecting her and apologizing if you've been too rough, you will begin to see a change. A woman is designed to respond to genuine love, which is why she can be so sensitive.

You also need to protect her emotionally. As I said before, she is a weaker vessel, and that includes her emotions. Let's use the analogy of a sensitive piece of equipment. I have grown up in and around the music and recording industry. I actually own different microphones, some inexpensive, and some very expensive. The inexpensive ones you can use for loud noises, such as a kick drum. The expensive ones are vocal mics. Due to their job, the less expensive ones are made tougher and are more durable. You can drop, kick, and abuse them, but they seem to keep right on performing.

However, my most expensive one is also the most valuable. It has its own foam lined box, and I loan it out to NO ONE! It has a gold plated diaphragm, and responds to a whisper. A kick drum could damage it easily, and hurt its performance. Its value is in its sensitivity, and I never want to destroy that. Too much spit can even hurt it so it even has a protective cover. I only take it out to record my voice.

This is your wife's heart. You can't treat her like you would a man. We can kick each other and use rough words, but we still bounce back. But if you treat your wife that way, you can damage her sensitivity, which is actually one of her greatest assets!

> *"Husbands, love your wives and do not be <u>bitter</u> toward them."*
>
> *Colossians 3:19 NKJV*

This scripture says it all. The word **bitter** here means to be acrid, which means sharp, pungent, or angry. I have to be careful because what seems normal to me may seem sharp, pungent, or angry to my wife. When we were first married, I remember going to fix a sandwich one day. I knew there was just enough ketchup left for one sandwich, because I had left the bottle in there the day before. When I looked, the bottle was gone and I asked my wife what had happened to the ketchup. She told me matter-of-factly that she had thrown it away. I said, "What? Why did you throw it away? There was enough for one more sandwich!" I'm not sure how I looked or sounded, but when I said that she started to cry! (I felt like Tom Hanks in the movie, *A League of their Own* when he said, "...there's no crying in baseball.")

I totally could not figure out why she would cry over that statement, so I asked her why she was crying, and she said, "Because you're mad at me!" I then tried to explain that I wasn't mad at her, just frustrated to be caught mid-sandwich with no condiment, but the damage was done, and I had to spend the next several minutes convincing her that everything was ok and our marital bliss was not over.

Of course she has grown over the years, and her sensitivities are more developed (you can get over-sensitive too, ladies), but I learned a valuable lesson that day. You can't treat her like a man during the day, and then want her to act like a woman at night!

Your wife also needs to find in you a sense of security. Just as children look to their natural fathers to get an idea about their

Heavenly Father, even so our wives look to our headship for the sense of security as a savior. He is our head and savior of the body, and in marriage, wives gain this same sense of God's headship and protection through us. Later on we will discuss the psychological and physiological differences between men and women, and it will help underscore this point.

For now let us understand that due to their emotional makeup, women are designed by God with the capacity to be more trusting. This goes back to the sensitivity issue that we talked about. They are designed by God to follow our lead, and it is amazing how far that will go. I have never ceased to be amazed at how a woman can stand by her man as Loretta Lynn crooned.

Unfortunately, this has been taken advantage of and abused, which in part gave rise to the feminist movement. Yes women can take a lot, (that must be why God didn't let men have babies), but there comes a breaking point. Their trusting nature can only be pushed so far, and as much as they can trust, once it is finally broken, they can put up walls that are almost impenetrable. I believe the only other emotional instinct that is stronger than this is the maternal instinct.

Due to this ability to trust, we must give them the sense of security that they need. I remember one time years ago when my father was going through a particular trial. I was concerned about him because he seemed to be more quiet and withdrawn. (This is usually our tendency; we as men close up to work out our problems.) I asked my mother what was wrong with dad, and she said he was working through some things, but she said, "I know your father; he will come through this and he will be fine. I just need to give him a little time." He of course did, and I am amazed at how his faith in God and resilience has brought him through many challenges in life.

But my point here is that my mother had a sense of security in his character. Even during financial challenges (with six children he faced a few) and the general challenges of life, she felt secure in his leadership, and along with her faith in the Lord, it kept her a woman of great peace. So make sure you create in your wife a sense of security. The best way is to have faith in God.

DIRECTION

The second responsibility the head has is for direction. We are to be the lookout for the body, and make wise choices for what's down the road. Too many times we fall back into maintenance mode, and the only direction we give is through the TV remote. Or we get shortsighted and want to make all the decisions in all the minor areas of life. There are many decisions your body makes all the time that you never have to think about. Aren't you glad you don't have to tell your body every time you need to breathe!

Often times our wives are far better managers than we are when it comes to the day-to-day operations. This does not mean that men are incapable of this, nor does it mean that women are incapable of making large decisions, but within a marriage someone must be responsible for the overall direction, and that is something that God has charged us with as husbands. The buck stops here!

God has charged us with the responsibility to look out for our families and plan for the future. For some this is difficult because they were never taught how. Some only know to work hard, and it will all turn out all right somehow. But we are responsible to educate ourselves and not cry that ignorance is bliss. Ignorance is, well, ignorant!

The key part of ignorance is *ignore*. How many times have we procrastinated on a job, say fixing a leaky roof, only to have the unpleasant revelation that instead of fixing itself, it only grew worse and more expensive! Ignorance is no excuse for failure, and we must take the responsibility of giving direction by becoming educated enough to have a direction. So how do we get direction?

> **"Delight yourself in the Lord, and He will give you the desires of your heart."**
> **Psalm 37:4 KJV**

Go back to God and ask Him to fill your heart with a fresh desire, a new dream. Put Him first and He will. Then start moving toward your dream. Even if it's stumbling at first, do what you know to do about what is in your heart. This is really a subject for another book, but remember, you can't steer a parked car! And don't complain that she won't support you in your dreams. (Nobody listens anyway, right?) Sometimes we need to man-up and give her something to follow. Have you ever tried to push a wet noodle?

In my years of counseling, one of the greatest frustrations I have ever dealt with is women whose husbands have no drive or vision! "Sheesh, why are you busting my chops, Pastor?" Because I know what pity does to a man. It slowly rots him to his core and steals all the opportunities that are staring him in the face. Besides, I'm just being a kick drum, and you're tough enough to handle it. You can thank me later, but right now get up and get a vision! You will be surprised how your wife will start getting behind you once you have a dream!

PROVISION

The area of provision is one of the most misunderstood areas of the responsibility of a husband. The number one thing to remember is, you are not the provider—God is. But as the head, it is your job to tap into that provision. Your main job is to obey God. Abraham was told one day to go and sacrifice his son Isaac. This was a test to see whether he loved the desire of his heart more than God.

To shorten the story, God commanded him to go to Mount Moriah and it was there at the place of obedience that he found his provision. God introduced himself to Abraham as Jehovah Jireh, meaning the one who's sees and makes a provision for you. So as a husband, know this: God has a provision for your vision! He will make a way for you when there seems to be no way. Be a man of faith and don't lose heart.

That doesn't mean it will always be easy. It took some effort to go to this mountain. He could have just gone to a closer, more convenient mountain, but there would have been no provision, and he might have lost his dream!

It was prophetically important to God that Abraham go to Mount Moriah, because it was there that God would later sacrifice His own Son for us! It is now the place of the temple mount in Jerusalem, and will be the future place from where Jesus will reign.

When you obey God, you are actually setting up your future kingdom! God's provision will be shown to you in the place of obedience and your family will benefit as well. Many men have gone through seasons of trial and lack, only because they disobeyed God or compromised in their obedience. The children of Israel wandered and a whole generation was lost through disobedience. So the most important part of fulfilling your responsibility of provision for your family is by being obedient to God.

To the ladies that may be reading this, make sure to always encourage your husband to obey the Lord. You may be forfeiting your own future by trying to steer your husband away from obeying God. Remember, God created Adam for Himself, and then created Eve to help him. They together were to serve God. We cannot become each other's idol. Even though your husband should have your interests at heart and your comfort above his own, make sure you are not making him follow your will instead of God's or you will be taking him away from that place of provision. Like Eve, you may just eat your way out of house and home!

Another facet of provision is financial planning. We must be good stewards, and cannot simply be foolish, or live paycheck-to-paycheck, even if the bills are getting paid. Your budget should allow for saving, miscellaneous spending, and such variables as will not put you under great financial pressure.

Faith is not buying something big on credit; it believes it in first and then spends it wisely. I am not saying it is a sin to have payments, but follow the proportion of your own faith. If you need to downsize to where your faith is, do it. Get to a place you can believe for and then go up from there. Too many people are writing checks their faith can't cash! Though all do not agree on the number one cause of divorce, most agree that financial pressure is at the top of the list.

Also, make sure you and your wife are in agreement. One or the other may have trouble believing, and if you are not in agreement it will hinder the faith of the one who believes, while tormenting the one who is struggling. It is not love to force your faith walk on your spouse, so GET THIS RIGHT!

Make sure you honor God *first* and that you are a tither and giver. Again another book, but God will honor those who **honor** Him, which means to put Him **first**.

> *"<u>Honor</u> the Lord with your possessions, and with the <u>first fruits</u> of all your increase."*
> **Proverbs 3:9 NKJV**

Second, make sure to budget properly. There are many great financial planning aids available. Stop thinking, "Can I make the payment?" Save, invest, pay cash, enjoy! You will be glad you did. Saving is not a lack of faith if it is not what you put your trust in. It is practicing good stewardship. Solomon continued by saying:

> *"So your <u>barns</u> will be filled with plenty, and your <u>vats</u> will overflow with new wine."*
> **Proverbs 3:10 NKJV**

Barns are for saving and **vats** for spending. He is saying here, "I will fill both your checking and savings account. If you will honor me, I will take care of you." This is also the reward of following wisdom. God can't bless either laziness or foolishness.

> *"But if anyone does not provide for his own, and especially for those of his household, he has denied the faith and is worse than an unbeliever."*
> **1Timothy 5:8 NKJV**

Laziness is not faith either. Don't use the excuse that you don't need to work because you have enough money. Do something productive with your life. The man in the Bible who said he would sit back and take his ease was not commended by Jesus, but was rather called a fool. Make your life count for something, and then you can enjoy the fruits of your labor.

A real question that comes up often is who should take care of the books. This is sometimes seen as "the man's job." The answer is simple: whoever is the best at it. I have seen it both ways. The important thing is that you are in agreement about your budget. I have seen disasters develop when one who has no ability takes charge of the money. People have gone downhill fast financially. However, that doesn't mean to put all the weight on the one doing the books. Communicate and agree on spending, and you will avoid needless frustration, and quite possibly divorce!

Another very important thing to remember is that you can't become a workaholic. I didn't say to be afraid of hard work, but don't let work become your supply. God is your provider. Some men work too long out of fear; others, to escape. But ether way is contrary to God's plan and is actually taking away from providing for your family in the emotional arena. Consider this verse:

> *"Do not wear yourself out to get rich; have the wisdom to show restraint."*
> *Proverbs 23:4 NIV*

Or as the New Living Translation says:

> *"…Be wise enough to know when to quit."*

There are three things that bring the proper balance to godly prosperity: **worship**, **wisdom**, and **work**.

Worship includes honoring God through your giving which results in God's blessing. Giving should always be an act of love and gratefulness to God, not a duty. God's response is a bountifulness of blessing that multiplies the harvest of your labor. *It's the right motive.*

> *"Honor the Lord with your possessions, and with the firstfruits of all your increase; so your barns will be filled with plenty, and your vats will overflow with new wine."*
>
> *Proverbs 3:9-10 NKJV*

> *"The blessing of the Lord makes one rich, and He adds no sorrow with it."*
>
> *Proverbs 10:22 NKJV*

Wisdom adds strength of character to knowledge and reaps great dividends. It brings diligence, consistency, and restraint to financial stewardship, resulting in investment and increase rather than mere consumption. *It's the right perspective.*

> *"Happy is the man who finds wisdom…Length of days is in her right hand, in her left hand riches and honor."*
>
> *Proverbs 3:13a, 16 NKJV*

Work is every man's responsibility. It is part of God's reward system, and is a true equalizer of man's effort. Reward is a motivator of action, and delivers us from the fallacy of the welfare state. *It's the right application.*

> *"In all labor there is profit."*
>
> *Proverbs 14:23a NKJV*

"For a dream comes with much business..."
Ecclesiastes 5:3a AMP

It's like a three-legged stool; you can only rest when all three legs are present. But when you forget one or the other two, you must overcompensate for the lack. Yes men do get rich by overworking, but they lose it through loss of health, or even lose the family they are working so hard for. So don't die young by overworking! Take a day of rest once a week, and make sure to thank God for your blessings. The more thankful you are, the less stressed you'll be.

Finally, when it comes to provision remember, money is not the only area. You also need to make sure your wife is ministered to emotionally. Just as we discussed spiritually your place, and financially your place, make sure you are ministering to her emotionally as well. Don't be so busy you forget either to pray together or play together. Money is a very cold bedfellow!

LEADERSHIP

You may think we have already discussed leadership when we discussed direction, and in a sense this whole book is about leadership. But the difference between direction and leadership is that true leadership produces the desire to follow. Someone once said, "If you are leading and nobody is following, you're on a walk."

You are only as good a leader as you are a follower. Leadership begins by how you follow God. Jesus only did what He saw His Father do. He was obedient even unto death, and He is now rewarded as no other, and given all authority in heaven and in earth. The better you learn to follow, the more you will understand what it takes to both follow and lead, and you will not only be entrusted with the greatest authority, but admired with the greatest respect.

It is also seen in how you follow those over you in life. It may be the boss on the job, or maybe your CO if you're in the military, or even in church for those who are charged to watch over your souls as one that must give an account. The Roman Centurion in Matthew chapter 8 made a powerful statement when he said:

> *"For I myself am a man <u>under authority</u>, and I have soldiers under me. I tell this one, 'Go' and he goes; and that one, 'come,' and he comes. I say to my servant, 'Do this,' and he does it."*
> **Matthew 8:9 NIV**

Notice how readily his soldiers and servants obeyed him? It stemmed from him being **under authority.** Men want their wives and children to give them obeisance, and yet when it comes to them, they are actually rebels, fighting against any restraint. Usually you end up seeing the worst rebellion in their own families. They open a door to rebellion and then use a heavy hand to drive it out of the ones under them. This is not leadership; this is despotism! It will destroy the ones under its grasp.

This leads to another area of leadership that absolutely affects your relationship with your wife: the children. Sometimes it is from a heavy-handed leadership that ignores her maternal instincts instead of factoring them in. Other times it is from the lack of leadership when it comes to the children. We are responsible as men, both to train up our children in the way they should go, and to bring them up in the nurture and admonition of the Lord. I like how the Message Bible puts it:

> *"Fathers, don't exasperate your children by coming down hard on them. Take them by the hand and lead them in the way of the Master."*
> **Ephesians 6:4 MSG**

Along with this, we are to back up our wife's authority. This is commonly understood by every authority structure in military and business alike. How frustrating if you are given a job to do, and then your boss won't back you up, or worse, lets you be the "bad guy" producing resentment in the employees under your management. This would be a major HR issue for sure! We have had more women in counseling sessions irate because their husband did not back them up with the kids. God is love, but He is also tough when He needs to be. You are not there to be their buddy; you are there to be the dad. Also, never undermine your wife's authority, or the wife her husband, in front of the children. They are smart and will intuitively read the weaknesses in the alliance to their fiendish little advantage!

The last area of leadership I want to touch on is that of your role as a team. Whether it is with decisions for the future, the children, or any matter of significance, make sure you are a team in your decision process. Like the speaker of the house, you are in leadership, but you need "buy in." Yes, there are times when you must "pull rank" again for emergency or necessity, but if you are wrong in your decisions and have made them unilaterally, you will bear the brunt of not only resentment, but lack of trust in your leadership.

Aside from that, it is always easier to get enthusiastic support if you will win your wife over through sharing your ideas, rather than running her over with your decision. A great leader will get those who follow to want to follow. A verse often used for soul winning is:

"...He who wins souls is wise."

Proverbs 11:30 NKJV

Your soul is defined as your mind, will, and emotions. A great leader will win the mind, will, and emotions of the team.

I remember one time when I was around twelve years old, my mother (who has now gone on to be with the Lord) wanted me to come and help her pull some weeds one day. We lived out in the country, and dad was often gone traveling in ministry. She had the authority to command me to help her, but she always had a way of getting you to want to help her. She first asked me with a cheerful look, as though she herself were excited about the task.

Then she gave me some vision. She said, "If we get this patch all cleared out, you will be able to play baseball out here." Now I loved playing baseball so I suddenly found myself working with greater endeavor, and calculating how far we had come, and how much longer it would take to clear the field. She had somehow managed to make the work fun. We worked together for hours that day and had a great time. She was a great leader, and a big influence on my life.

That is what a great leader does. They inspire the team unto greatness. They collaborate and share the rewards together. So my advice is, don't just make unilateral decisions and inform her, or worse, just let her find out later (guilty), but include her in the process. Always get your wife's perspective on any major decisions, or any decisions that will affect her. I have never made any decision of consequence without my wife's agreement. This has served me well and kept me out of a lot of trouble. What a foolish general that won't listen to his advisors!

That sensitivity issue that we spoke of now comes back into play. Many a time my wife has had the intuitive read on people and has saved me from much heartache. This does not mean I abdicate the throne either, for I will be accountable for my own decisions; but like Ecclesiastes says:

"Two are better than one; Because they will have a good reward for their labor."
                    Ecclesiastes 4:9 NKJV

We could go so many directions with this thought, but suffice to say, value your wife greatly, listen to her advice and perspective. The life you save may be your own!

CHAPTER 5

THE MAN IN THE MIRROR

W hat do you see when you look in the mirror? I'm not talking about your self-image, your character or any of the deep inward parts, but the literal reflection. There are five things I want you to focus on so you can know how to treat your wife. Every morning when you shave, this will be a reminder so you can not only treat her right, but also keep your prayers from being hindered. I want to focus on five main parts of the head: the **eyes**, **ears**, **nose**, **mouth**, and **chin**.

THE EYES

The first part of the head I want to focus on is the eyes. Let them remind you that you need to be a visionary. You need to be one who looks ahead and prepares for danger. Eyes need to be open. Eyes need to be both near and farsighted. Eyes have peripheral vision to catch things and see the big picture. Eyes can focus the attention. All of these abilities need to be utilized on behalf of your wife. There are so many analogies here that I'd like you to stop and make a quick list on your own of how your eyes apply to your relationship with your wife.

Here's one example: Your eyes are meant to notice her. I love nothing more than just to look up from what I'm doing when my wife walks in the room, and just stare at her until she realizes that she is more important than my work, the ball game, or anything else in my life at that moment. Then I smile at her and tell her with my eyes that I am in love and captivated by her beauty.

You have no idea what it means to your wife to know that you notice her. That's why it's so important that you notice when she gets her hair done, or buys a new outfit. They are looking for a sense of approval, and that you like what you see. This shows them that you care about them enough to take note of the details. Remember, if you don't some smooth operator will be happy to take your place. Don't let her natural desire to please you become discouraged and then end up being fulfilled by someone else! My wife's book gives some illustrations on that one.

You also need to use your eyes to look into your wife's soul. It is said that the eyes are the windows of the soul, and when you look with love, you can see things in your wife's eyes. When something is bothering my wife, I can always see it in her eyes. When I say, "What's wrong?" and she responds, "Nothing," I can be foolish and ignore it, or I can look in her eyes and know to dig deeper. "Let sleeping dogs lie" you may say, but you are simply building a bigger wall to deal with later, so don't ignore it. Look into her eyes until you see love and peace there.

THE EARS

The next part of the head is the ears. Our ears remind us that our wife needs to be heard. This is one of the most important things we need to give to our wife. But it is more than a "Yes dear," as you allow her to ramble on while your mind is elsewhere. You must give her your full attention.

If you are anything like me, sometimes I can get so focused and one-track minded that I will carry on a conversation with her and later realize I haven't the foggiest idea what we just discussed or I agreed to. When this is happening, we have worked out a little thing between us. I told her it is like I am in one file working and she brings up another file. So her little catch phrase is, "I need to pull your file," which is my cue to put down what I am doing and give her my full attention. She is telling me, "I need your ears and your brain attached. I need an intelligent conversation." Because she is the most important thing in my life, she should always get my attention. (And because I'm the most important person in hers, she always tries to find the best time to interrupt me.)

It is also important to remember that we have two ears and one mouth for a reason. (Ok, it's for the brain to judge distance through the stereophonic auditory pattern; don't be so technical.) But seriously, our wives need to share the details. It is important to them and whether you realize it or not, it is important to you.

I must admit I am still working on my doctorate with this one. I am a bottom line kind of person when it comes to communication. Just give me the facts and I can draw my own conclusions. Just tell me the street name and left or right, don't tell me "it's after the big red barn past the silver silo, then look for the dancing cow and turn there."

God has given us something valuable if we will just take the time to listen. It is in our wife's communication style that our lives become intertwined, emotionally mixed and blended until we learn to share life on a deeper level than just facts. We are more than just computers. A great cook can take all the ingredients (facts) and blend them into something that is satisfying to the taste. A great pianist can take the 88 keys and make them into a symphonic blend of sound. Any man can make a piece of toast or play chopsticks, but a woman can take life and make it a masterpiece. Let her! (I am repenting in my mind already.)

It's like shopping. I hate it. But to my wife, it's hunting! One day God grabbed my attention as I was whining about how long a particular shopping excursion was taking and He said to me, "You don't have to enjoy shopping; just enjoy that she enjoys shopping." I stopped looking at my watch and just began to marvel as she went from rack to rack, holding things up, checking out prices, looking for sales. I became enraptured with her enjoyment and found that I actually enjoyed being with her! (She reminds me of this from time to time.)

But let's get back to listening (thanks for pulling my file). Make sure you don't try to solve all her problems. Usually she already knows what to do. She doesn't need the answers, she just needs to know you care she is having a problem! You see, men and women blow off steam and relieve emotional pressure in different ways. Men...we *hit* things. But women...they relieve pressure with words. (Now tell me which one sounds more intelligent.) It's that "testosterone vs. estrogen" thing - more on that later.

Listen like a wine taster. They don't just gulp it down already knowing how they will judge the taste. They first cleanse the palate so that their taste buds are not tainted. Next they examine the color, and swirl for viscosity. With a whiff they take in the bouquet and savor the aroma. Then with a sip they allow it to rest gently upon the tongue until each sense of taste has fully awakened and grasped the full body of flavor. And finally they swallow it down allowing its warmth to be felt upon the cheek. OK, so that's way too many words for a bottom line communicator, but you get the picture. Prepare yourself to listen. Drink in her words as though you were savoring a fine wine, and try to connect to how she feels about what she is saying. And don't get discouraged about this, it is an acquired skill. It's like fishing or hunting; you improve with practice until you become an old pro. I'm still practicing.

THE MOUTH

Again, this is a most important part of the head. Your wife needs your words. Did you hear me; she *needs* your WORDS...like you *need* SEX! She needs to hear you say, "I love you! You are beautiful!" "Wow, honey, you smell great!" "Thank you for dinner, it was great!" "Thanks for all the time you spend taking care of the family!" And so on, and so on...

In the great book, *His Needs, Her Needs* by Willard F. Harley Jr., there is a list of the top five needs of men vs. the top five needs of women in marriage. I'll bet you can guess men's top need right off the bat. Yes, sex. It is a God-given drive that is partially due to the high level of testosterone in our bodies.

But for women, that didn't even make the list. Their number one need is affection, and number two is conversation. [2] Studies have shown that conversation to a woman releases hormones in a woman's brain that give her the sensation of taking drugs. [3] They have more brain cells devoted to speech and conversation than men. Like I said, they *need* conversation like we *need* sex.

The problem is that we try to apply the golden rule, do unto your wife, as you would have her do unto you! We need to operate the golden rule, but in this sense, meet her needs as a woman, just as you would have her meet your needs as a man. It again brings in that principle of sowing and reaping. Just like anything, you get out what you put in.

We have some very dear friends that are pastors who also minister on the subject of marriage. They have a unique perspective because theirs was all but destroyed, and God put it back together again. We actually walked through some of this with them, and believe me, their marriage looked like it was beyond repair. Humpty Dumpty had nothing on them. But God gave them a revelation about the power of words, and it changed their marriage and their lives.

You see he is very much a man's man in the sense of tough and gruff. She grew up with a father that was very expressive and outwardly affectionate. She tells the story of how her mother would buy a new dress, and when she walked in the room, her father would make a big scene about how beautiful she looked. One day just like her mother had for her father, she had also gotten a new outfit, and had spent much time fixing herself up, and was anxious to show it off for her husband. But when she walked in the room and waited for him to say something, he just looked at her. She said, "Well?" and he said, "Well, what?" Then she said, "I got a new outfit. How does it look?" To which he replied, "I don't have a problem with it." NOT the response she was looking for at all! This was an example of how his lack of words slowly wore her down until she was emotionally bankrupt, and wanted out.

Then God gave them a tremendous revelation out of the Bible:

> *"Husbands, love your wives, even as Christ also loved the church, and gave himself for it; That he might sanctify and cleanse it with the <u>washing of water by the word.</u>"*
>
> *Ephesians 5:25-26 KJV*

Although he was a wonderful man of God, and would speak God's word, he didn't realize that he was not **washing her with his words,** just like Christ washes us. As he began to put this principle into practice, God began to slowly undo the damage that was done. He truly repented in his heart, and asked her forgiveness, and God gave her the desire to try again. They are now deeply in love with a wonderful marriage, so never think you are too far gone for God's power and the power of words.

This is how we need to wash our wives. We aren't talking a spit bath here. We are talking a bathtub full of words. Your words cleanse and heal your wife. They minister to her in a way that brings her comfort and even a "harmonic" euphoria. So give her your words in the same measure you would like to have sex! It actually ministers to your wife, and washes away all the negative words, feelings, and experiences of her day!

THE NOSE

They say the nose knows. I don't know who *they* are and I was unable to confirm this through my research. However, it is claimed by some that the nose actually has the ability to find magnetic north? Supposedly there is a magnetic sense that is stronger in some than others to find magnetic north. My sister-in-law claims this ability, and has demonstrated it on occasion. I, on the other hand, am directionally challenged. But one thing is for certain, the nose can smell things and that is a crucial sense. It can let us know when food is bad, and can save our life. It is an ability to perceive things, or we could say discern.

In the natural, a woman's sense of smell is much more highly developed than that of a man. But we have a responsibility as the head to discern things, to "sniff things out" as it were. Just as our nose can protect our stomach from something harmful, we are supposed to protect our wives from harm.

Too bad Adam didn't do this in the garden! Eve gets a bad rap when it comes to the fall of man. She is portrayed as the temptress who lured him into sin through her wily ways. But the fault was really Adam's! He was the one who was to blame by not protecting her from deception. Consider the following verses:

> *"But I fear, lest by any means, as the <u>serpent beguiled Eve through his subtlety</u>, so your minds should be corrupted from the simplicity that is in Christ."*
> > *II Corinthians 11:3 KJV*

> *"<u>And Adam was not deceived</u>, but the <u>woman being deceived</u> was in the transgression."*
> > *I Timothy 2:14 KJV*

Eve was deceived by the subtlety of the serpent, but Adam's job was to protect the garden. Yet instead of casting out that serpent and washing Eve with God's word (Satan misquoted what God said and twisted the meaning), Adam **partook** of the fruit:

> *"And when the woman saw that the tree was good for food, and that it was pleasant to the eyes, and a tree to be desired to make one wise, she took of the*

fruit thereof, and did eat, and gave also <u>unto her husband with her; and <u>he did eat</u>."</u>

Genesis 3:6 KJV

Did you notice it says he was **with** her? He had the responsibility to stop her and cast that old serpent out, but instead he left the spiritual responsibility to her, and later blamed God for giving her to him. We cannot abdicate our throne and them blame it on our wife or on God. It is up to us to be the ones who know the Word and protect our families. We have the authority to cast the old serpent out of the garden of our homes. Therefore we need to protect our wives through our discernment.

THE CHIN

As I was thinking about this analogy to remind us of our headship responsibilities, the chin came to mind. It is because we need to be the ones who can, "take it on the chin." The chin is a feature of the face that gets the moniker as being strong. A masculine look is supposed to have a square jaw and jutting chin. Those who are considered with a weak chin are those who sport more of the "turtle neck" feature (sorry, Barney Fife). A boxer is said to have a weak chin if he is easily knocked out. This phrase is actually an English idiom and defined thusly, "If you take it on the chin, something bad happens to you and you take it directly without fuss."

This is our job as men. When danger or difficulty comes, we are to be the ones who step out in front and take it like a man! This is again the reason God gave us the testosterone packed response.

We can see this demonstrated in many areas. We must know how to protect our wives from well meaning in-laws.

"For this cause shall a man <u>leave</u> his father and mother, and shall be joined unto his wife, and they two shall be one flesh."
Ephesians 5:31 KJV

We are to **leave** and cleave. No apron strings here! Although you should always honor your father and mother, you have now started a new family and thus, next to God, you have a new first allegiance: your wife! You need to stand up if your wife is attacked in any way and from any source, including both of your sets of parents. Do it in a respectful manner, but protect your wife and stand up for her. You may get some negative reaction, but just take it on the chin! It will blow over, and you will establish boundaries and actually gain respect if done properly.

If you are a parent and reading this, for the love of your kids, leave them alone! Be there for them of course, and be ready to offer advice if asked, but don't try to run their lives. They are not children any more, and must have boundaries. A man can't leave his father and mother too well if they won't leave him alone. This has actually resulted in the destruction of marriages, so trust God and let them live their lives, mistakes and all. Of course you can voice your concerns, but approach them the way you would a good friend. This will keep them from resenting you and actually going the opposite way.

Now, for all the mama's boys out there, don't compare your wife to your mother!!! Don't compare her cooking, her house cleaning, or anything else for that matter. You didn't marry your mother. And don't complain to your mother about your wife. This will only breed resentment. There are only three people you should talk to concerning your wife: God, your wife, and your pastor or counselor. When you complain to friends or family, they may resent them because of their affection for you, and though you may forgive, they may not as easily. If you are in a situation that requires others to be involved, make sure you also follow up with them and tell them you have worked things out, and share your culpability in the matter. That way forgiveness can go around and all will be reconciled.

The final and one of the most important areas is with your children. Should you meander down the pathway to starting a family, there are some things you should know. Those little angels have horns! Of course we are all born with a sinful nature, which is self-centered and wants what it wants when it wants it. This is why we have to train up our children.

> *"Foolishness is bound in the heart of a child; but the rod of correction shall drive it far from him."*
> *Proverbs 22:15 KJV*

No doubt our children do not like this process, and they will do whatever they can to bypass this, including manipulation, tantrums, and pitting one parent against another. None of these worked in my house, because my father would not allow it. We were trained that to employ these tactics would not get the desired results. Obedience was far more rewarding! But one of the main reasons this worked was because my mother and father backed each other up fully. I can not remember one incident where they disagreed in front of us as children. The other reason it worked so well was because my father stood behind my mother implicitly. We were more afraid of disobeying her for fear of his anger in doing so, and would never dream of sassing her for that same reason. We knew dad loved us, but we also knew he loved mom, and she was there first.

Some parents like to be the good guy, and will leave all discipline to the other parent. This is a cop out and is extremely unfair. It's also not really loving either your spouse or your children.

It is especially distasteful when it is the husband not protecting the wife. The Bible tells us that God is love, but it also teaches that we should fear the Lord, and that the reverential fear of the Lord is the beginning of knowledge. Although the wife is given authority as the "despot of the house," the husband's ultimate authority needs to back this up. It is our task to **train** and **discipline** our children.

> *"<u>Fathers</u>, do not provoke your children to anger, but bring them up in the <u>discipline and instruction</u> of the Lord."*
>
> *Ephesians 6:4 NAS*

> *"For whom the LORD loves he corrects; Just as a <u>father</u> the son in whom he delights."*
>
> *Proverbs 3:12 NKJV*

So if you love your children and you love your wife, you will be the one to lay down the law, and to back up your wife when she enforces it. Never, and I mean never, allow your children to disrespect your wife. There were times when our children were growing up that either my wife or I had been under too much stress and were not handling the discipline the best. So the other one would step in and say, "Why don't you let me handle this one," or "Let's go in the bedroom and discuss this." Either way we were supporting one another and not letting the kids see any division. United we stand.

CHAPTER 6

UNDERSTANDING
YOUR WIFE

There is much that has been said about the feminine mystique. "You can't live with 'em, and you can't live without 'em," "It's a woman's prerogative to change her mind," and such like. But is it impossible to understand a woman? Doubtless, there are as many arguments on the other side that it is we men that are the difficult ones. Books such as, *Men are from Mars, Women are from Venus* [4] do a good job at describing the real issue: we are different! Some have tried to attribute the differences merely to environment, how we are raised, and societal issues, but science is beginning to confirm what God knew all along. We are wired differently.

Of course we can see the obvious physical differences. I don't know about you, but I am very thankful for the differences!

CAN I SEE THOSE BOTTLES?

Years ago when my oldest son was about two years old, we had some friends over to the house. They recently had a baby, and my friend's wife was breastfeeding at the time. During their visit their little one let us know in no uncertain terms that it was mealtime. She found a comfortable chair in our living room, and proceeded to nurse the baby, and my son happened in the room. She was draped in a blanket, but told us that he curiously walked up to her and with a quizzical look asked, "What are those under there?" She told him, "Those are the baby's bottles." She said he thought for a second, and then leaning down he asked, "Can I see those bottles?"

We men are all alike. We learn from an early age that there are differences between the sexes. I'm sure every one of you has a story of your curious years. My sister and I were little more than a year apart, and I remember trying to figure out why she didn't have all her parts yet. That curiosity is innocent and absolutely normal, but there are more differences about us than just our physiques. Our wives want us to be interested in more than just "seeing their bottles."

DWELL WITH THEM ACCORDING TO KNOWLEDGE

We cannot use the excuse that women are too hard to understand. It is really a cop-out. What we are really saying is that we don't want to put in the effort. But God doesn't give us this out.

> *"Likewise, ye husbands, dwell with them according to <u>knowledge</u>...."*
> *I Peter 3:7a KJV*

God wants us to have **knowledge** about our wives. The more knowledge we have the more we will understand them. The more we understand them, the less frustrated (and frustrating) we will be. The less frustration there is, the more we will enjoy our lives together. So, where to begin...how about the obvious?

PHYSIOLOGICAL AND PSYCHOLOGICAL DIFFERENCES

Again, we know that we are physically different. It is so amazing (and wonderful) how God made us to be the perfect fit! When God said that He would make a **help meet** for Adam, He literally meant the perfect fit.

> *"And the LORD God said, It is not good that the man should be alone; I will make him an <u>help meet</u> for him."*
>
> *Genesis 2:18 KJV*

That King James Old English word **meet** means *to fit*, the way that gears mesh together. This was not just talking about our bodies, but our whole spirit, soul, and body relationship.

Some say that opposites attract, but I believe that opposites balance. Our strengths as men and women complement each other and make the perfect team. Too bad sin entered in and selfishness got involved. It has made a tug-of-war out of the differences, when God intended them to make things better. This is why we need God in our marriages. God is love, and love causes us to see each other as a blessing instead of a curse.

This perfect fit, of course, includes our bodies. Though our bodies fit together perfectly, they operate very differently. The primary difference is due to the different levels of testosterone and estrogen that make up our bodies. These chemicals affect us from the cellular level and even effect how our brains develop and operate.

We are uniquely male and female from the earliest stages of development. When sex is determined and testosterone is released in the embryo, it starts affecting the formation of the male brain. The amount of cells designated for the speech, emotion, and memory sections of the brain are reduced, as well as the cerebral area. This is why men tend to be less emotional and more distant when working out their issues. The opposite is true for the female brain. The female brain has more cells given to the functions of speech and emotion. Therefore they are more expressive and emotional by nature. [5]

The release of testosterone also increases the part of the brain that controls sex drive in men as well. Men think of sex an average of once every 52 seconds, while women think about it once a day. [5] It's a good thing or we'd never get anything done! Some scientists disagree with this and say that there is no difference between the amount of words that men and women speak. I wonder what planet they are from?

Men tend to use mostly the left brain to process things, while women use both sides. The left brain is the logical side. The area of the brain that deals with mathematics is typically larger in men as well, causing them to score consistently higher in math. (Einstein's brain was found to be abnormally large in this area.) A woman has a larger right side of the brain which is much more sensory in nature. [6]

FILTERED OR NON-FILTERED

Once, while on a plane, I read a study from a scientific magazine on the way men's and women's brains respond to stimuli. They hooked up their brains and then showed each one the same series of pictures. What was interesting was the response that the brain activity registered when they saw pictures of a traumatic nature. When men saw the picture, it first registered in the logic portion of the brain, and then went to the emotion center. But when they showed the same picture to the women, it first passed through the emotion center, and then on to the logic portion. This again underscores the emotional filter that women use when processing things. Doesn't that make sense?

To illustrate this point, it's interesting to note that most men will ask the question, "What do you *think* about..." but most women will ask, "How do you *feel* about..." Both are using reason, but the female mind first wants to process the emotional impact of a subject, where a man wants to process the logical side of an issue.

I have to laugh here at myself, because I just looked back at that last paragraph and read what I wrote, "Doesn't that make sense?" That's the issue—we want everything to make sense! We think women are so illogical! (Our Mr. Spock ears are showing!!) They feel we are sometimes so callous and uncaring. But don't you see how that life requires both perceptions, and just like the eyes seeing the same thing from slightly different angles, we get a better perception of life, and are a great balance. Don't try to make a man out of your wife, and ladies, don't try to make a woman out of your husband.

My wife is funny. She can't cut up a whole chicken because it looks like a baby to her. It makes her feel bad. It looks like a chicken to me and I have no problem wringing its neck. Not inhumanely, but sorry animal activists, I am just helping that chicken fulfill its destiny. While there may be some women who have no problem with the chicken issue, and some men who do, there is still a general difference in the way we process things, and that difference is good.

WOMEN ARE BETTER CAREGIVERS

Due to a larger, deep limbic system, women are much more able to be in touch with the emotional side, making them able to make bonds easier, which makes them better natural caregivers. [6] This is why it's good for women to raise the children especially when the children are younger. They are just plain better at it than men. There is much scientific knowledge to back up the importance of having both a husband and a wife to raise the children. This shoots holes in the new definitions that are being placed upon the American family. And isn't it amazing that science backs up the Bible perfectly in all these areas.

The limbic system difference also makes women more susceptible to depression and anxiety issues, which would explain post-partum depression, among other things. This shows us the importance of being the head as we discussed earlier, and the need for us to use our words to build up our wives. Now don't you ladies just give in to depression, and don't let the devil exploit this area of your make-up. But men, don't get irritated that they don't just roll with the punches like you do. Build them up and cover them in prayer. That's your part as a husband.

There is also a difference between how men and women respond to pressure. Men usually get angry first, and will try to use force, but when broken, they may cry. Women will usually cry first, but when pushed too far will get angry. This is because the response when logic is challenged is frustration that leads to anger, but the response of emotion when challenged is tears. So you need to let your wife cry when she feels like crying or she may get angry! And you know the old saying, "If mamma ain't happy, ain't nobody happy!" (On a picture in my pastor's house the next line says, "If daddy ain't happy, nobody cares.")

MONTHLY CYCLES

Of course this is another way that men differ from women. Men, it is very important that we give a wide berth here. Unless you have had a period, you have no right to tell your wife how to act on her period. The fact is that women's bodies differ from one another in this area, and all respond differently. But there are some general similarities that it would be good for you to understand:

1. It is hormonal! Yes, you knew that, but understand what hormones are. They are chemicals in the body. Drugs are chemicals and can alter how people act, even beyond their control.

2. It is emotional! Yes, you knew that too. But these emotions can vary, from anger to tears, and again these can seem irrational because they are hormonally based, not logically based. Don't expect it to make sense.

3. It is painful! This pain can range from the dull ache to sharp pain and nausea with moderate to severe headaches. Imagine having a week long toothache, with times of sharp, shooting pains that you can't rub or ease. Have compassion, and just thank the Lord you don't have to deal with this.

4. It is synchronized! Did you know that when women are in proximity, their periods tend to synchronize with each other? No it's not a conspiracy to gang up on you. In fact, it's probably good, especially if you have daughters. Can you imagine if you had three daughters and your wife all having periods on different weeks?

5. It intensifies a woman's desire to have sex! You didn't see that one coming did you? While we are pretty much 24/7 when it comes to our desires, woman are cyclical, and their desire increases as their period subsides. This gives the best chance for those wanting to get pregnant, and can really unleash the tigress in your wife! (All the more reason to treat her well during this week.)

Make sure to give extra care to your wife if she is trying to get pregnant. If she has her period, not only is this disappointing, but due to the hormonal issues it is easier for depression to try to sneak in. Make sure you build your wife up, and that doesn't mean tell her that she needs to just get in faith. Faith works by love!

Also, some women's cycles are like clockwork, and some are more erratic than others. Just look for the signs and act accordingly. Signs can be irritation, fatigue, soreness of breasts, and crying. Be sensitive and you'll both survive.

MENOPAUSE

This time of transition in a woman's life needs your special understanding. Some women look forward to passing this milestone because it marks the end of the monthly cycle. Others dread it because it makes them feel older. This time can be a bumpy ride, but like going through clouds in an airplane, it's sunny and clear on the other side, and can lead to a real freedom and potentially rewarding time of life.

Menopause starts usually between the age of 45-55, and on average at 51.4 years of age; however, it can occur as early as the 30's and as late as the 60's.[7]

Menopause is considered to be officially entered after at least 12 months without having a period. The transition time is known as premenopausal, and is the time when we associate the many symptoms including hot flashes, night sweats, erratic periods, and a host of other issues, one of which is increase in facial hair and lowering of the voice. This is due to the hormonal balance changing. The benefits include a newfound freedom and increase in sexual desire for the woman once menopause is reached. Again, this can be a challenging time, so be sensitive to the unique needs of your wife.

MAN CAVE VS. WOMEN'S CLUB

These physiological differences help to explain the desire of men to retreat into our man cave and work things out, while women want to call up a girlfriend and talk it out. But as we've stated in a previous chapter, she needs to talk to you as well. We have covered that need sufficiently, so let me just say here, that it is still important for each of us to have our male/female time. Just make sure it's balanced. Your wife needs time with the girls, and you need your man time. The danger for women is the gossip circle, and the danger for men is the loner cycle. Women can be susceptible to the enemy planting thoughts in their mind that you don't love them, and that can sometimes be exacerbated by the local women's circle. Even more deadly is the man cave that gets infiltrated by the pornography trap. We'll revisit that issue in chapter ten. Suffice to say, keep things in balance and make sure to fulfill each other's needs. The best defense is a strong offense!

This is where communication is vital. Eighty-seven percent of those who seek divorce say that the main reason is deficient communication.[8] I encourage you to get a book devoted entirely to communication, for that is a subject in itself. (Check out, "Now You're Speaking My Language" by Gary Chapman.) But let me give you just a few hints for good communication:

1. Pick a time that's good for both (Not while either is under pressure)
2. Prepare yourself before you talk ("Clear the palate")
3. Make eye contact without distractions
4. Listen intently (It must be two-way communication)
5. Ask questions and clarify ("So you're saying this?")
6. Be consistent (Daily talk time, weekly date night)
7. Get past the surface (Make sure you get to the issues that matter)

If you will make the time to talk and make sure not to let resentments build, you will keep a healthy and growing relationship. It's like your car; if you don't maintain it, eventually you will have some pretty big repair bills. Maintenance is far cheaper than procrastination, and far less painful.

There are other physiological differences that we will discuss in the next chapter.

CHAPTER 7

FULFILLING YOUR WIFE SEXUALLY

D o you realize that the very first command of God to man was to have sex? And it was a blessing for both of them!!

"So God created man in his own image, in the image of God created he him; male and female created he them. And God blessed them, and God said unto them, 'Be fruitful, and multiply, and replenish the earth'...."

Genesis 1:27-28 KJV

Sex is God's idea. He created it for three main reasons: intimacy, pleasure, and procreation. What an amazing day that first day must have been for Adam and Eve. Adam had spent the morning naming the animals, and then God said, "Take a nap, I've got a surprise for you!" While he was sleeping, God took from his own flesh and formed a woman. The Hebrew words for when He made Adam and Eve are different. The word for making Adam meant to "roughly squeeze together." Adam was "chiseled." But the word for making Eve literally meant "formed or handcrafted." Eve was "built!" What a birthday present! She was one of a kind, and that has always been God's intent, that we have that one and only someone to spend our lives with.

So there they were; the first couple on their honeymoon in paradise! I don't think there has ever been a love scene written that could have equaled that day. They were naked and had nothing to be ashamed of. As I stated earlier, sex was God's idea, God's wedding gift! There was nothing shameful or wrong in it. There was no sin to cloud its purpose, no guilt to lessen its climax, and no fear to hinder its expression. It was a beautiful spiritual moment, a soul satisfying, and physically euphoric fulfillment of what God intended it to be: the closest and strongest bonding of two human beings in the covenant of their marriage before Him.

THE COVENANT OF MARRIAGE

Before you can truly understand the importance and purpose of sex, you must understand the marriage covenant. Marriage itself is an institution of God, and He has passed the care and oversight of it to the church. It is a covenant between a man and woman that was never intended to be broken. It is a sacred vow to God that must be honored at all costs. Men, we are first and foremost children of God, and He is giving us permission to marry and bond with one of His daughters for life. This is a great privilege.

I have a beautiful daughter of my own. One day some young man will come and ask my permission to marry her and I am going to want to know that he is pledging his life for her future well-being. I am going to require a level of character in him to prove this to me. It is because I love my daughter with all my heart and I want her to be fulfilled and happy, and she is worth more to me than all I possess. This is how God feels.

THE BLESSING OF THE COVENANT

This is why the marriage covenant is so important. God gives you this great privilege of marrying His daughter, and then promises or covenants with you to bless you. There is a special blessing of God on marriage, and this is why people should never just live together. Not only are they cheapening the covenant and ignoring the Father's will, but they are also cutting themselves off from the Father's blessing!

It is the same when you betray the covenant. God's blessing is withheld, and your favor departs.

Consider these verses:

> *"...You fill the place of worship with your whining and sniveling because you don't get what you want from God. Do you know why? Simple. Because God was there as a witness when you spoke your marriage vows to your young bride, and now you've broken those vows, broken the faith-bond with your vowed companion, your covenant wife. God, not you, made marriage. His Spirit inhabits even the smallest details of marriage. And what does He want from marriage? Children of God, that's what. So guard the spirit of marriage within you. Don't cheat on your spouse."*
>
> *Malachi 2:13-15 MSG*

Breaking your vows includes everything from treating your wife roughly, to lusting after another woman in your heart, to pornography, to adultery, to unjust divorce. It cuts off the favor of God and stops your blessings from flowing. IT'S NOT WORTH IT!! Repent and make it right. Run from the very thought of another woman, and into the arms of your wife. Take her by the hand, get on your knees before God, and renew your vows.

If you've already gone through a divorce that was your fault, you need to repent to the Lord, and if possible, to your ex-spouse. Ask Him to remove the curse off of your life and restore the blessing. This will allow you to start anew and move forward. Thank God for the blood of Jesus!

Sexual Union and the Covenant

Not only is marriage a sacred covenant, sex is the consummation of that covenant and is also sacred. Sadly to say, sexual union has been so cheapened in our society today. Sex was meant to be the bond of the covenant, and it takes over our whole spirit, soul, and body. So powerful was this bond to be, that it affected us not just on a physical level, but an emotional and spiritual one as well. Casual sex requires the destruction of our soul and the sacrifice of our emotion. It was never intended to be a test drive. It is the blessing that goes with the covenant of marriage; the reward of faithfulness to that covenant.

A covenant is far more than a mere contract, which is a legal agreement between people, and can be broken for various legal reasons. A covenant is a life pact, an agreement with God and your mate, based upon life-vows, which are meant to be unbreakable. You are making a vow directly to God, and to break it is tantamount to high treason. These vows were only to be broken by death itself, or released if one party broke that covenant through sexual infidelity with another. This was God's original beautiful picture.

SEX IS FOR MUTUAL FULFILLMENT AND TO BE ENJOYED!

Although sex itself is sacred, within the marriage covenant it is completely free, and intended to be experienced to the ultimate!

> *"Marriage is <u>honorable</u> in all, and the bed <u>undefiled</u>..."*
>
> *Hebrews 13:4a KJV*

The Greek word for **honorable** here means to be "valuable, costly, beloved and precious," and its root word gives the connotation of a reward. **Undefiled** here means to be pure, or literally without shame. [9] The bed is God's reward for your vow of faithfulness, and sexual fulfillment is completely blessed and condoned by God Himself. This is why sex should never be used as a weapon. It is defrauding to withhold sexual gratification from your mate. It is part of your covenant before God that you give your body to your mate in marriage, and it is your responsibility to fulfill your mate's sexual needs. I have found that most men agree whole-heartedly with this, but have actually had instances where men were not fulfilling their part.

> *"Let the husband <u>render unto the wife due benevolence</u>: and likewise also the wife unto the husband. The wife hath not power of her own body, but the husband: and likewise also the husband hath not power of his own body, but the wife. Defraud ye not one the other, except it be with consent for a time, that ye may give yourselves to fasting and prayer; and come together again, that Satan tempt you not for your incontinency."*
>
> *I Corinthians 7:3-5 KJV*

I know this is King James, but I find it humorous how these men in the middle ages described this command. "**Render unto the wife due benevolence.**" It sounds so formal, but it literal means, "*Give up the goods!*" It is a command to fulfill your wife sexually and satisfy her physical wants and desires. You are not the only one who has a sexual appetite. Yours may be more readily apparent, but hers is more enduring. Look at nature itself. Male sperm swim faster, but don't last as long. A man has one orgasm and he has to wait to reload. Women can have multiple orgasms. Why would God give them this ability if He did not want it fulfilled?

Notice he speaks to the husband first. I believe it is our responsibility to make sure our wives are fulfilled before we think about ourselves. I don't mean who reaches a climax first. I mean that we make sure our wives are satisfied sexually. And to a woman, sex is the whole experience including romance, foreplay, pleasuring, and ultimately orgasm. We men are a "one trick pony." It's all about the climax. But for women, there is arousal and euphoria in the romance of sex, as much as in the physical release. It's up to her to decide which is more important, and when she is satisfied. It's like going to a baseball game. Some fans only enjoy when the team scores a home run, while others enjoy the whole experience from singing, "Take me out to the ball game" to the seventh inning stretch. Men want to score, and women want to enjoy the experience. The point is, both are supposed to enjoy the game!

Notice also that sex is never to be abstained from in a marriage except in the case of mutual agreement to focus on fasting and prayer. I never deny my wife even if I am on a fast, unless she is in agreement with it. This is to keep the devil from having an open door to tempt one or the other. There's way too much temptation in the world today, but it's a lot easier to be tempted when you are starving than when you are full, sexually I mean. It is also a command to reunite sexually after abstinence. Whoever said Christianity was prudish didn't have a clue! In fact, if you read my wife's book, sex is meant for daily recreation if you can handle it!

God commands us to have sex when we are married, and it is a danger sign when sexual relations breakdown. It is a code red to a marriage, and the root issues need to be resolved so things can move forward. Don't settle for a marriage without sex! Get help immediately, from a trusted Christian source, and kick the devil out of your bedroom!

THREE LEVELS OF SEXUAL FULFILLMENT

The problem is not that women don't want sex. The problem is that they *do* want love, and many men don't know how to express it! Sex needs to mean something to a woman, and it is more difficult for them to become aroused if there is an emotional block or a spiritual wall.

Again, we are three part beings; spirit, soul, and body. Sex is actually designed to affect us in all three levels: *physical*, *emotional*, and *spiritual*.

PHYSICAL SEX

Physical sex is actually the lowest level of fulfillment. That doesn't make it evil, and we should be completely satisfied physically. However, a truth remains: flesh is never satisfied.

For example, have you ever wandered into the kitchen looking for something to eat, and nothing seemed to do the trick. Many times what we think is physical hunger is actually something deeper. The purely physical sexual appetite is never completely satisfied or no man would ever be attracted to anyone but his wife. And yet, pornography is a multi-billion dollar industry. It's because flesh alone is only about personal gratification. Our flesh should be fed and taken care of, but it is the higher parts of man that separate us from the animals. Our soul and spirit were meant to govern our flesh. The soul deals with what is fair, and the spirit with right and wrong.

Animals have natural instinct, but they have no law of conscience, and weren't intended to. We, on the other hand, can enjoy life on a higher level; and things like honor, duty, and love are just some of the things that give a deep sense of satisfaction that is never known on a mere fleshly level. So physical sex is good, and when governed by marriage, is totally right, legal, and viable. But sex even in marriage can be empty if it is not shared on a deeper level.

Women get this. A big part of that is the physiological differences we discussed in the previous chapter. Because men's main pleasure sensors are released through sex and adrenaline creating activity due to our testosterone makeup, we have the strongest physical drive, and thus pursue physical intimacy. This is good and designed by God so that intimacy would be pursued. But there are levels of relationship more important than sex, and more fulfilling when added to sex.

There are levels of friendship that go deeper than the rush of endorphins at sexual release. Men who have fought together in war have a deep bond, which is why movies like *Braveheart* are so popular among men. You are giving yourself for something greater than yourself, and like the famous line from that movie, "All men die. Not all men really live."

David and Jonathan had that kind of deep friendship in the Bible, and that prompted the statement that love of their friendship was, "greater than the love of women." Some have tried to twist this passage to mean that they had homosexual sex, but they were describing a level of friendship that would lay down his life for his friend. This is a deeper love that is past the self-preservation appetites of the flesh. Remember, it is not wrong that you have an appetite for sex, any more than that you have an appetite for food. Food propagates your life, and sex propagates the human race, and so God gave natural appetites to assure these things, but physical sex is the lower level.

EMOTIONAL SEX

The next level is that of the soul. This is the part of us that has reason, emotion, and will. Just as God designed in the man to have a sex drive, He knew in His wisdom that we need emotional and soul-level fulfillment.

Again due to the physiological differences, God designed that the woman would help to balance the man, by making her brain, due to estrogen, to desire emotional intimacy on a stronger level. Here is the key to why romance is so important to a woman. They are wired with a need for social intimacy and fulfillment. This is not to say that men are void of this, or that women are void of passion. Do you want your wife to be more passionate? It is locked behind door number one, and the key is romance! Is it any wonder that romance novels are such a huge industry!! A woman wants the door of her sexual passions unlocked, but cannot be aroused when locked behind the doors of pent up emotion. Behind that door rests a wildly passionate woman. Why not be the prince that fights the dragon, climbs the castle, and unlocks the door to your princess.

As frustrated as men get with the issue of erectile dysfunction, I believe that many women are suffering from their own form of ED, it's called *emotional dysfunction*. Unfortunately, it is many times brought on by our lack of attention and or understanding of those needs. It's time we became the emotional "Viagra®" that she needs through caring, sharing, and hearing her, until the blockage to her own sexual release is removed and then look out boy, she'll wear you out!

This level of sexual fulfillment also deals with our intellect, and there is something to be said about intellectual stimulation. A woman is aroused that her husband has a plan, has good ambitions, and betters himself intellectually. Some men who are only after their own appetites prefer the "dumb blonde" stereotype (my apologies to blondes).

A woman wants to know you are interested in her intellectually, because she is after all, anything but dumb. Women have been put down because they have a strong sense of emotion, and it is true that sometimes emotion can blind reason, but this does not make them dumb by any means. I see emotional sensitivity as a strong asset, and it's a vital factor in dealing with human relationships.

Mr. Executive, you need someone who has a keen instinct of people to make the most informed decision, which is why Ms. Executive is now emerging in the areas of business. (By the way, Proverbs 31 describes a modern woman who not only cares for her family, but owns and operates her own business as well.) Nothing is more frustrating to a woman than being marginalized by a man simply because she is a woman and he is a man.

So when you have enough respect for your wife to value her intellectual aspects uniquely balanced by her emotional perspective, you will not only benefit immensely from her contributions, but also unlock the doors of her desire to be sexually responsive to you.

SPIRITUAL SEX

The highest level of sexual fulfillment is the spiritual level. This is the level of pure love. It is so focused on your mate being fulfilled that you forget about your own needs. This makes sense, because God is love, and we are made whole when we are spiritually made right with Him. This level of your being is found in your conscience and intuition, and it is key to how you govern your own life.

When you are spiritually in tune with God, you are clean from sin, free in your conscience, and can know intuitively because you are unclouded in your thoughts and motives. Guilty consciences automatically become self-focused.

This is what the knowledge of good and evil in the Garden of Eden was all about. It wasn't about God hiding knowledge from Adam and Eve. He was already like God, made in His image, and had access to all the knowledge of the universe that was good. It was that God was protecting them from the realm of sin, guilt, and shame, and all of the damage that it does to us both mentally and physically. You don't have the knowledge of good until you have the knowledge of evil, because everything is good; you just have the knowledge of *being*. God is the great I AM, and man was created an "I am" as well. Good was just normal, and everything was good. Sin brings death because the conscience is clouded and cut off from God. Fear entered in through sin, and fear is one of the worst limiters there is to man's abilities. Perfect love casts out all fear, and that's why God sent His Son to die for us. Only God was still sinless, that's why a man could not pay for his own sins. There was no way to cleanse his own conscience once he had sinned. It was now an indelible mark. But Jesus came to free us in our conscience, and He created the path of restoration through reconciliation with God.

Now bring that revelation into the marriage bed. When sex is the expression this kind of love that is so focused on fulfilling the other person, it starts the wonderful chain reaction of sowing and reaping the desire in the other to reciprocate.

When you are at peace in your own conscience with God, that proverbial "hole in the soul" is filled. You stop trying to fill it with other things. There is a satisfaction of living and just "being" that all the money in the world can't fill. All the sex, drugs, toys, or any other thing pale in comparison to this inward peace. That is found in Jesus, the Prince of Peace, God's Messiah who came to save us from our sins. (If you do not know Him, stop right now and ask Him to forgive you of all your sins. Repent to Him for living life your own way, and be reconciled to your creator. You will find the beginning of this peace, and believe me; it will find its way all the way back to your bedroom!)

It is a known fact in our house, that after we have a really great service at church, it is usually the best sex that we enjoy together. It is from that sense of oneness and fulfillment with God.

CHAPTER 8

KNOWING YOUR WIFE

I t's such an interesting thing to me that God used the word "know" to describe sexual union in the Bible. It really captures the concept that we discussed in the last chapter; that sex is more than just physical. However, you can't consummate that union without physically affirming what your heart and your mind feel. In order to "render due benevolence" you really need to "know" your wife, top to bottom.

I'm sure you already know the birds and bees basics. I actually looked forward to sharing these wonderful facts of life with my sons. Sex isn't dirty, I taught them, but it is very special and personal. But to be honest, I didn't really know all that I could have when I got married.

My father's generation was not as open, and though he gave me all the information I needed to know to make babies, my wife had to fill me in on all the details. (And I didn't mind a bit.) I am embarrassed to say, but I didn't even know that women could have an orgasm, let alone multiple. It is a sad fact that in many marriages, there are women who have never had an orgasm. Some women don't care, but I think it is important to do things according to the designer's specifications. Besides, seeing your mate reach a climax is part of the enjoyment of this great and wondrous bonding experience, and so it is for your mate as well.

Of course sex begins with an understanding about the body. I'm going to assume you know how yours works by now, so let's move on to the female anatomy. Song of Solomon is a wonderful biblical book when it comes to being descriptive of the beauty God created in a woman's body. (It wouldn't hurt to take some lessons from Solomon about how to talk to your wife either – the book's initials are S.O.S. for those of you who need a little help!) His description of the female anatomy starts from the top and works its way down, enjoying every part like a beautiful panorama, literally from head to toe in Chapter Four, and from toe to head in Chapter Seven. Look at his poetic description in this second passage,

> *"How beautiful are thy feet with shoes, O prince's daughter! the joints of thy thighs are like jewels, the work of the hands of a cunning workman. Thy navel is like a round goblet, which wanteth not liquor: thy belly is like an heap of wheat set about with lilies. Thy two breasts are like two young roes that are twins. Thy neck is as a tower of ivory; thine eyes like the fishpools in Heshbon, by the gate of Bathrabbim: thy nose is as the tower of Lebanon which looketh toward Damascus. Thine head upon thee is like Carmel, and the hair of thine head like purple; the king is held in the galleries."*
>
> *Song of Solomon 7:1-5 KJV*

There's more to your wife's body than just the "T & A," buddy! (With language like that, it's no wonder some men don't get sex as often as they want.)

SEXUALITY AND SENSUALITY

It is very important for a woman to feel sexy, and the bedroom is the place for that (or wherever you can find your privacy). Women are beautiful by design, and there is nothing wrong with looking sexy privately. There is a difference between being attractive and being alluring.

In public, you can look attractive, but sexy and alluring is for the bedroom and for the husband alone. When it comes to dressing in public, men, don't have your wife dress trashy, and ladies don't buy some of the present trends to look sexy. Dressing sexy in public usually comes from being insecure and needing attention or acceptance. You need to make your wife feel very secure and sexy at home, so she doesn't need anyone else to fill that emotional tank. Some men want their wives to look sexy in public for their own ego, and to prove they can get someone that "hot." This is selfish and not protective of your wife. Ladies, you can be very attractive and modest at the same time. But when it comes to the bedroom, you can be as sexy as you want to be.

God made our bodies to be enjoyed with each other. Make sure you tell your wife she looks sexy, men. Remember the importance of your words, and how they actually give a similar euphoria to a woman. This will help to start the sexual desire in a woman.

Sensuality is attached to the senses. It is the joining of our five senses to our sexuality, and employing them for the purpose of making love. Sensuality really heightens sexuality, and can bring the experience to a new level. Sensuality is increased the more other thoughts and distractions are decreased. It is the transition of the brain from focusing on tasks and details of life, to focusing on the experience of making love.

For a woman, certain senses are naturally stronger than men. Their sense of smell is much stronger, and so it is very important for things to be clean and smell nice or she can be distracted and the sexual connections diminished.

Mood music helps us with the sense of hearing, and can cause relaxation, which aids in the release of tension and yielding to the experience. It's called getting in the mood, and it is very important to the woman's body, especially when is comes to her natural lubrication. Just as a man must be aroused to have an erection, a woman must be aroused to become wet. (This process is more natural just after her period, and diminishes more as her period approaches. Synthetic lubrication is sometimes necessary.)

The sense of taste is important, and of course there is a natural desire in women for chocolate. The debate about whether or not it is an aphrodisiac still goes on, but there are at least three chemicals in chocolate that are similar to the effects of certain drugs, and have a positive effect on the sense of well being and elation.[10] The bottom line is that women enjoy it, and accompanying that sense of joy to the pleasures of sex causes at least an emotional tie-in to the joy of sex.

Sight is very important too, and women have a great sense of beauty. Taking them to romantic places to eat with a beautiful view and a great ambiance helps fill this sense for beauty. Once you get back to your private room, make sure she has something more than your holey underwear to look at. (Definitely not a time to be holier than thou!) A fun date can be going underwear shopping together, and pick out what you would like each other to wear.

Also, make sure to pick up after yourself in the bedroom. Picking up around the house is not just a "woman's job," especially if you both work outside the home. Sharing duties or helping her pick up, relieves her mind of that sense that things don't look good. You don't want anything to distract her senses and refocus them on tasks.

The sense of touch is one of the most important. Men get turned on by sight, but woman are much more moved by touch. The sense of touch is not just with the hands, but every square inch of the body.

Certain parts of the body are very sensitive to touch. These parts of the body are called "erogenous zones." The word *erogenous* comes from two Greek words, *eros* and *genous* which literally means the "birthplace of passion." That is why foreplay is so important because it is really the "birthplace of passion," especially for women.

Though some of these zones are the same for men and women, certain areas are uniquely more sensitive in men vs. women. Common areas are the fingers, nipples, and buttocks. For men, the genital area is the most sensitive (duh), but for women, although the genital area is very sensitive, other areas are very sensuous and important in giving her pleasure. These areas include the ears, neck, armpits, navel, and inner thighs.[11]

Men may enjoy going straight for the target, but for women, it is important that you visit these other zones before going for "home base." Remember, her body (and brain) has to prepare to open up and receive you, and this is somewhat like a combination lock. By stimulating these areas you are telling her brain and body to "prepare for arrival." It helps her feel you are not skipping from "first base" to "home plate" which can cause a disconnect and leave more of a feeling of being used. Their bodies have no time to respond and produce natural lubrication, making penetration painful, and reinforcing the subconscious feeling that sex in not enjoyable. It can become another mental roadblock resulting in less frequent sex. (You don't want that do you?) Just as you need to be stimulated for an erection, she needs to be stimulated for penetration, and love will take the time.

Here's a helpful hint to remember for both of you: "When foreplay is longer, orgasms are stronger." Maybe that will help you understand the importance of not just rushing through.

No wonder the Pointer Sisters sang the song *Slow Hand*. Read these lyrics, because they really echo much of what we just said:

Slow Hand
Pointer Sisters

As the midnight moon, was drifting through
The lazy sway of the trees
I saw the look in your eyes, lookin' into mine
Seeing what you wanted to see
Darlin' don't say a word, cause I already heard
What your body's sayin' to mine
I'm tired of fast moves
I've got a slow groove...
On my mind

I want a man with a slow hand
I want a lover with an easy touch
I want somebody who will spend some time
Not come and go in a heated rush
I want somebody who will understand
When it comes to love, I want a slow hand

On shadowed ground, with no one around
And a blanket of stars in our eyes
We are drifting free, like two lost leaves

On the crazy wind of the night
Darlin', don't say a word, 'cause I already heard
What your body's sayin' to mine
If I want it all night
You say it's alright
We got the time

'Cause I got a man with a slow hand
I got a lover with an easy touch
I found somebody who will spend some time
Not come and go in a heated rush
I found somebody who will understand
When it comes to love, I want a slow hand. (12)

Did you get that? "I want somebody who will understand." I actually began to weep when I read those words and realized how many women are crying out for their husbands to understand them, and to really love them. How many times have they said inside, "I'm tired of fast moves, I just wish my husband would take the time to see me, to notice me, to care for me."

Stop and pray this prayer right now with me:

"Oh God in heaven, it is my prayer that I will come to realize what a gift you have given me in my wife, and to love her like you want me to love her. Forgive me for neglecting to understand her, and help me to make the time that I should for her. Help me to fulfill her needs spirit, soul, and body, and help us to discover the depths of what sex was intended to be. In Jesus' Name, Amen."

I believe that even with this prayer, you have begun a road of healing and new discovery for you and your wife.

CHAPTER 9

THE FEMALE ANATOMY: ENJOYING THE JOURNEY

We can continue now with the female anatomy, and perhaps add to your knowledge concerning your wife's uniquely female parts. (I will be discussing some things in detail, so fasten your seatbelts!)

Once you have taken the time to visit all the erogenous zones, your focus naturally turns to the areas we, as men, would be attracted to the most, starting with the breasts. I once heard it said, "You know why God gave women two breasts? Because He gave men two hands!"

A woman's breasts are a very special place of love. It is very natural for a woman to want to draw near to her breasts the one she loves. Lay your head down and just listen to her heart beat.

> *"A bundle of myrrh is my well beloved unto me; he shall lie all night betwixt my breasts."*
> **Song of Solomon 1:13 KJV**

You can look at, fondle, kiss, and caress her breasts. They are yours to enjoy! But your wife also should enjoy your attention. Be gentle because there are times her breasts can be sore, such as prior to or during her period. Remember, the nipples of both men and women are especially sensitive. God created these areas and He intended them to be enjoyed. Ask your wife to tell you when she enjoys something, but make sure you are not just working out a formula. She may enjoy it this time, but may enjoy something else another time.

Moving a little further south, a woman's entire midriff from her navel to her thighs is her **"goblet of wine, and garden of spices."**

> *"Thy navel is like a round <u>goblet</u>, which wanteth not liquor: thy belly is like an heap of wheat set about with lilies."*
>
> *Song of Solomon 7:2 KJV*

> *"Awake, O north wind; and come, thou south; blow upon my <u>garden</u>, that the <u>spices</u> thereof may flow out. Let my beloved come into his <u>garden</u>, and eat his pleasant fruits."*
>
> *Song of Solomon 4:16 KJV*

As previously stated, the naval is a sensitive area, and one of the erogenous zones for a woman. Your wife may enjoy you kissing and touching her sensitive areas. The imagery is that of becoming drunk on her love. The vaginal area is important for us to understand. The hooded area at the top of the vaginal opening is the clitoris, and is especially sensitive. You may want your wife to direct you on how hard to press or rub on this area. It is important to spend enough time in foreplay to bring your wife to a place where she is ready to proceed. She is capable by God's design to have multiple orgasms, so if she desires, fulfill her desire.

At this point let me address something that is a question to many. What about oral stimulation? My wife covers this in her book quite thoroughly, so I will sum it up in this manner. The Bible does not address this directly, therefore it is left up to the conscience of the couple to decide. Some feel this is wrong, and therefore should follow their conscience. However, others feel completely free to express their love in this manner. The only area directly addressed and condemned in the Bible is sodomy.

Medically speaking, the male and female genital areas are completely safe and considered sterile, as much as any other part of the body when bathed, unless a disease is already present. The anal area is bacterial, and penetration can cause damage, as well as damage the sphincter muscles. Nature itself gives us warning here.

The two things to keep in mind are the law of conscience and the law of love. Always go by the weaker conscience. Love will never force your mate to do anything that would be contrary to their conscience.

The vaginal opening is surrounded by labia or vaginal "lips" and when aroused these will swell with blood and become wet with the body's natural lubrication. This is, of course, to prepare for penetration; however your wife may continue to enjoy foreplay.

One of the big questions is the famed "G" spot. Just inside the vaginal opening approximately one or two inches up against the pubic bone is an area that can produce a strong contraction when orgasm is reached. The best thing to do is to allow your wife to direct you toward what pleases her physically. Don't get hung up on trying to find the "G" spot. Just make sure you are focusing on the "L" spot: love!

One more thing to remember; your wife can reach multiple orgasms if she desires, and it doesn't have to only be with your penis penetrating her vagina. You can help her find pleasure in any way that is within your conscience and comfort zone. (And she for you as well.)

THE JOURNEY

Now that we have discussed your wife's zones and anatomy, let's focus on the actual journey of giving her satisfaction. There is no "right way" or "road map," just an application of the things learned in whatever order or way that you personally desire together.

Of course, not all rendezvous can last for hours, and there is nothing wrong with a "quickie" of pleasuring either one, or the other, or both of you. There is also no set rule as to the time of day or frequency. As my wife teaches, the Bible says as often as daily, so it is up to the couple. You are in more danger of not having sex enough than you are at having it too much. But you need to make sure your wife is satisfied, and you should find time at least once a week to have true, genuine, face-to-face intercourse. Remember, God commanded it!

So here are some thoughts for you as you bond together. Start with her hair. Women spend thousands of dollars on hair products because their hair is very important to them. Take time to notice it; the style, the texture. Make sure to find out if your wife likes you to play with her hair. The scalp is sensitive, and can be a sensuous area as well. You may want to give your wife a head and neck massage. This can help her relax and release tension. (Perhaps you have already drawn her a bath, and allowed her some personal time while you put the kids to bed, or do the dishes.)

Spend some time taking in the beauty of her face. Look into her eyes as pools of water. Memorize their color, the length of her lashes. Caress her brow, her cheek. Take time to kiss her lips. Not just a "simulated sex" French kiss, or the "suck her lips off her face" kind that TV portrays. You may get to that as passion stirs, but a woman loves to be kissed out of love and genuine affection.

> *"Let him kiss me with the kisses of his mouth — for your love is better than wine."*
> **Song of Solomon 1:2 NKJV**

Whisper into her ear, take some time to kiss (and nibble if she likes) her ears and neck. Use your fingers, maybe the back of your hand to brush gently her jaw line and down her neck to her shoulders. Take it all in! You may even use something soft to heighten her senses. It's allowed! You have a covenant, and God is pleased for you two to have pleasure in His gift.

Continue on ministering to all five of her senses. Ask what she is in the mood for, and don't get your feelings hurt if she doesn't like a particular thing. Just move on to the next. If there seems to be resistance, ask her if there is anything she needs to talk about. She may say no at first, but make sure, and grow sensitive spiritually with her.

I can always tell when something is bothering my wife. Many times we have started to make love, and I have sensed something blocking the way. Usually taking time to minister to her and listen to her talk removes the block from her mind, and ends up being some of the best times of lovemaking. Elvis had it wrong: A little *more* conversation, a little more action!

I'll add here too, that I have been asked, "Is it ok to talk dirty?" Sex is not dirty! Verbalization can fulfill the sense of hearing in your mate, and erotic verbal expression is absolutely fine as long as you don't go against your conscience. We usually call it dirty because we have been ashamed about sex. It is only wrong outside of marriage. The devil, not God, is the one who either wants to pervert sex, or keep married people from enjoying it. (1Timothy 4:1-4 calls "forbidding to marry" a "doctrine of devils.") Satan would love to limit married couples from enjoying this wonderful gift. Jesus said it this way:

> *"The thief's purpose is to steal and kill and destroy.*
> *My purpose is to give life in all its fullness."*
> **John 10:10 NLT**

If Jesus is Lord of our whole life, that includes an abundant sex life!

Continue the journey and take the time to enjoy the view along the way. Look at Solomon's description of a journey of love:

> *"How fair and how pleasant art thou, O love, for delights! This thy stature is like to a palm tree, and thy breasts to clusters of grapes. I said, I will go up to the palm tree, I will take hold of the boughs thereof: now also thy breasts shall be as clusters of the vine, and the smell of thy nose like apples; And the roof of thy mouth like the best wine for my beloved, that goeth down sweetly, causing the lips of those that are asleep to speak."*
> **Song of Solomon 7:6-9 KJV**

There are so many expressions of love and emotion, and yours is a lifetime to explore each and every avenue together. You may have different moods on different nights. You may feel funny and goofy; or serious and somber. You may feel romantic; or steamy and passionate. Whatever mood, whatever delight or expression, God has blessed you with this wonderful intimacy of love.

CHAPTER 10

SLAYING THE DRAGON: BREAKING THE POWER OF PORNOGRAPHY

One of the greatest dangers to the foundation of our society is the blight of pornography. It is feeding an ever-growing addiction, and perverting the beauty and wonder of this gift of sex into an ugly and ever-twisted, descending spiral of moral decay.

I believe it is time for men to stand up and rescue society from this evil. It is time for Prince Charming to slay the dragon and deliver the damsel from the distress of being objectified instead of valued and loved. For anyone to say at this point that such a statement is prudish and old fashioned, they obviously have skipped the previous few chapters of this book. Let's look at the nature of this beast.

Pornography comes from the Greek root word *porneuo* - meaning: to act the harlot, fornication, adultery or incest of either sex. It is defined literally in the World English Dictionary as, "writings, pictures, films, etc., designed to stimulate sexual excitement."[13] It is a multi-billion dollar industry that has become epidemic in its addictive abuse, and has destroyed marriages, fed sexual addictions, and perverted the nature of sex.

Many have failed to see the damage this can do. Some "experts" say it is a healthy way to jump-start a stale sex life. It is prescribed by some therapists to help overcome erectile dysfunction. Society today has thrown behind them the instructions from the very One who created them and knows how best they operate.

With all we have seen about God, and knowing that He designed sex for our benefit, it doesn't compute to think that His ways would be harmful, outdated, or restrictive. Yes, there are restrictions, but those are for our safety and to preserve our ability to enjoy sexual fulfillment for life.

First of all, Jesus made it very clear that to **lust** is a sin.

> *"But I say to you, that whoever looks at a woman to lust for her has already committed adultery with her in his heart."*
> *Matthew 5:28 NKJV*

One commentary reads that the definition of lusting is to look with continual longing with the mind made up to commit the act if at all possible. This does not mean if you happen to see it, but if your intent is to act upon it. Temptation isn't in and of itself a sin, but acting on it is. Like someone once said, "You can't help it if a bird flies over your head, but you don't have to let it make a nest in your hair."

But the important thing is that you can commit the sin in your heart even before acting upon it. Adultery is a terrible sin that is directly against the covenant you made with God and your mate. All sin brings death, and many fail to see the consequences of that sin. Let's examine some of the dangers and destruction pornography can cause.

DAMAGED RELATIONSHIPS

One thing is that it damages your relationship with your wife. Even if it is a hidden thing, it causes you to begin to desire the pornography more than the real thing. It is intimacy without effort, and though that may seem tempting, it is like living in space. With no gravity, you become weaker until there is no more strength and your bones literally turn to powder. We have already seen the necessity for personal intimacy, and the effort it takes to be intimate with your wife is beneficial and vital.

It steals your emotional and spiritual fulfillment. Remember sex is on three levels. What happens is that one is heightened at the expense of the other two. The problem is that the flesh can never get satisfied, and will always demand more. This is why pornography slowly pulls you into deeper perversion ending in the inability to be fulfilled. Like a drug addict, all you care about is more, until you can't be satisfied with any.

It is an incredible time and talent waster. People will get lost for hours, until every spare minute they have is consumed with seeking the fix. So much energy and creativity is lost, not to mention falling behind on responsibilities.

There is a danger that other family members may fall into it, either by coming across the "secret stash" or by the influence of leaving that spiritual door open. Men measure the psychological aspects, but there is a spiritual realm and demonic influences that seek to ensnare and captivate human beings through their own weaknesses.

LOSS OF EXCITEMENT AND FULFILLMENT

I'll bet this is one area you didn't think of, but there is a danger of being "over-exposed" (no pun intended) to pornography; that of loss of excitement and sexual fulfillment. Remember this principle; sin always costs you more than you want to pay!

> *"For the wages of sin is death…"*
> **Romans 6:23 KJV**

Sin will always destroy something. It will always cost you something; and the cost is always far more than the perceived benefit. Though it promises freedom, it will end in bondage. Though it is fun for a season, in the end it will always bring pain.

Let me give you an example. Someone could say to you, "It's a lot of fun to quit paying your bills! It's so free to just take your paycheck and spend it on whatever you want!!" Though it may feel that way, just wait until the creditors begin to catch up to you. Talk about the hounds of hell!! They won't leave you alone until they have taken the last possession you own. They will repossess everything you once enjoyed. It would be better by far to do it the old-fashioned way of faithful stewardship and wisdom. Then you will be able to spend freely, and enjoy the financial freedom.

Why is it that we can accept this when it comes to money, but throw away all common sense as "prudish, old-fashioned, superstitious, religious nonsense" when it comes to the tried and true expressions of marital monogamy?

So here is just another way that your enjoyment of sex is diminished; overexposure leads to the need for more stimulation to reach the same level of enjoyment. In other words, when you see too much sexual stimulation without the need to pursue your wife, it takes more and more to, shall we say, "rise to the occasion." I don't want to get bored with my wife's body!! I want it to be a wonderful delight every time I see her! It's no wonder that Viagra® is flying off the shelves.

Look at a recent question I found on a blog:

> *"I usually look at porn and masturbate every evening before going to bed. Can this desensitize me and make me not get aroused as easily when making out and having sex with girls? If this is true, which I am starting to believe, then I'll of course stop immediately."*[14]

The answers were all various personal opinions, but all of them agreed that it would definitely to one degree or another affect a person in this way. (Interestingly enough the blogger's online moniker included "cantsleep.")

Another blogger wrote:

> *"Hey, I have had some exotic sexual preferences in terms of porn & after not being able to perform with a girl it seems a very good idea to cut it out for good. My question is, how long before my sexual arousal returns to normal? Should I cut masturbation out altogether for a while to speed up the process? I am confident that this is the real problem, so please no pro porn arguments! Thanks."*

This was from the question titled, "Desensitized by porn? How long to re-sensitize?" asked on answers.com, and the most popular response was voted as follows:

> *"Yes, I think you have desensitized yourself. This can usually happen when you use a method that really*

arouses you, which can also be things like sex toys, and of course porn. This might be hard (no pun intended) but you should try not to look at porn for a few days to a couple of weeks, and not masturbate as well. This will slowly bring up your sex drive again and shouldn't really have a problem performing with your girlfriend again. Hope it goes well for you."[15]

Though I disagree that simply cutting back on the porn will solve the issue, not to mention the lack of having a marital covenant (again the emotional and spiritual means of fulfillment from the last chapter), this goes to show the public experience and opinion regarding the subject. While it is not on the level of a scientific study, personal experience does merit some level of understanding.

Another response from this thread brought up the issue of masturbation to porn:

"Making a habit of masturbating at porn and finding more and more exciting videos as the old ones tend to bring less and less arousal causes sexual desensitization over a long period of time. This is because the brain gets used to your own ways of reaching climax (i.e. porn & masturbation) so you will become less impressed by real women - they are now too vanilla for you compared to what you have experienced via porn. It is somehow like drugs. First it brings you virtual joy and then, over years, it gives you real pain because being unable to perform with real women can be devastating for a man's psyche..." [15]

This was voted second highest reader rating. Now let's look at what experts are saying. According to a report on pornography and cybersex, authors Gene McConnell and Keith Campbell point out that there are five stages of-porn addiction: early exposure; addiction; escalation; desensitization; and finally acting out sexually.[16] The first seems harmless enough as natural male curiosity is fed through initial exposure to pornography. But this appetite becomes a personal replacement therapy to natural relationships and addiction is born. Now these last three phases begin to subtly and increasingly take hold. The escalation phase is the same as a drug addict, when lesser drugs are not able to produce the same high as before and stronger stimuli is sought out. In other words, "soft" porn no longer satisfies, and the danger signs of conscience are ignored, causing further desensitization and resulting in the addict to seek more "hardcore" abuse of human sexuality.

This constant barrage of images produces the ultimate desensitization that leads to less ability to become aroused, erectile dysfunction, and emotional disconnection; a high price to pay for what began as a "cheap" thrill that "really doesn't hurt anybody." It is now a web that has established brain patterns and taken over the physical reward system that intimacy with your mate was intended to be. It becomes an insidious control used by the very enemy of your soul to steal what God so beautifully intended.

This ultimately leads to the most damaging phase, which is acting out sexually. The images are not enough, and now a physical target is sought out, willing or unwilling in their participation in this uncontrollable urge for sexual fulfillment. What promised such freedom of pleasure has now resulted in slavery.

PORNOGRAPHY AND ERECTILE DYSFUNCTION

It is heartbreaking as a pastor to read thread after thread of men crying out due to their inability to have an erection with the one they love. Over and over they report that due to pornography and masturbation, they cannot become aroused no matter how badly they desire it. Though many would become stimulated by the porn, the "real thing" was unable to produce any stimulation. Some "experts" would say then to use porn for stimulation, and then climax with your "significant other." But time after time the responses of others would come back that the only thing that restored their ability to find meaningful sex with their mate was to break the "self medication" of pornography and masturbation. One reader responded that breaking away from these completely followed by a time of bonding emotionally with their woman was the key to "resetting" their brain to normal, and finding fulfillment once again.

Here is one example found on a thread on the website medhelp. org of a young man with similar issues:

"To: BananaJoe, bummed_out, all

I've been looking at porn since I was 9. I'm 21 now. It's only during the last year, once I started to get seriously sexually active that I realized I had an ED problem. After going through the requisite freaking out about how I was too young to have ED and embarrassment when I couldn't just pop up and go the way guys my age are supposed to be able to, I began to suspect there was some connection to porn. I have no problems when watching porn, but I'm dead when it comes to me being with my girlfriend. And I love her.

It is scary how little awareness there is on the net that ED caused by too much porn is a very real problem. It's not about us lacking confidence, or being uneasy around our lovers, I truly believe its all about desensitization. Although my heart and soul are in my lover, she just can't physically arouse me. She can't compete no girl can ever compete, with the endless sexual visual fiction porn offers.

So, after reading through a lot of similar stories on medhelp, I've decided to give up porn and hope that my penis starts functioning normally, with the girl I love, and not with meaningless fantasies online.

BananaJoe, your story is truly a source of faith for me that my problems can be worked out. It's been 3 days since I've been off porn, and will be visiting my girlfriend at her home in Colorado in three weeks. I hope years and years of visual desensitization and addiction aren't going to destroy my chance to ever have a normal sex life.

Ps - I think we really owe a round of thanks to the wonderful women in our lives who have stood by us while we face our worst fears and wrangle with this debilitating embarrassment. I hope for all of you to have a supportive girl in your life as I do."[17]

This is the cry of so many. And do you see what the real desire is? It is intimacy with the one they love. Even then, there is a complete loss of the importance of marriage itself. God knew what He was doing when He established the covenant of marriage and the blessing of sexual consummation to that covenant. This man, as most others I read were simply seeking to re-establish the emotional level of fulfillment, not even realizing that there is a spiritual level beyond that, which belongs only to those who will commit to one another in the covenant of marriage. Some may argue that their bond is just as spiritual, but they are discounting the effect of the blessing of God that true freedom of conscience can bring. There is a oneness that you can have with your mate, that nothing else can match or replace.

Although pornography may be an effortless thrill at first, it will cost you your conscience, soul, emotion, and intimacy, and will enslave you with a lack of true fulfillment. It is like the adrenaline rush of stealing to a thief. The "heist" has to become larger until no amount satisfies. That is the trap of sin, and the only real cure is repentance to God and your mate, and true forgiveness and restoration.

Pornography can never replace intimacy, because a picture will never love you for who you are.

FINANCIAL DESTRUCTION

There is another spiritual principle that many men don't realize when they participate in this sin: it opens the door to financial struggle and ruin. Remember, Jesus taught that looking to lust is the **same as adultery**.

> *"...Whoever looks at a woman to lust for her has <u>already committed adultery</u> with her in his heart."*
> *Matthew 5:28 NKJV*

Now consider this:

> *"My son, pay attention to my wisdom; listen carefully to my wise counsel...The lips of an immoral woman are as sweet as honey, and her mouth is smoother than oil. But the result is as bitter as poison, sharp as a double-edged sword. Her feet go down to death; her steps lead straight to the grave. For she does not care about the path to life. She staggers down a crooked trail and doesn't even realize where it leads...Run from her! Don't go near the door of her house! If you do, you will lose your <u>honor</u> and hand over to merciless people everything you have achieved in life. Strangers will obtain your <u>wealth</u>, and someone else will enjoy the fruit of your <u>labor</u>.*
> *Proverbs 5:1, 3-6, 8-10 NLT*

Do you see that! You will lose your **honor, wealth,** and **wages.** This is a spiritual principle, and is sometimes the reason that people can't seem to escape financial struggle. Yes, God forgives you when you ask Him to, but every event is a new opportunity for the devil to steal from you.

And continuing:

> *"And you mourn at last, when your flesh and your body are consumed."*
> *Proverbs 5:11 NKJV*

It even opens the door to sickness. Literally we see STDs and AIDS resulting from following through with the outward act, but the sin opens the door for you to be attacked.

God's answer to pornography and any sexual lust is:

> *"Drink water from your own cistern, And running water from your own <u>well</u>. Should your <u>fountains</u> be dispersed abroad, Streams of water in the streets? Let them be only your own, And not for strangers with you. Let your <u>fountain</u> be blessed, And rejoice with the wife of your youth. As a loving deer and a graceful doe, Let her breasts satisfy you at all times; And always be enraptured with her love."*
> *Proverbs 5:15-19 NKJV*

The **well** is your wife and you are the **fountain.** Enjoy the gift God has given you and stay full of her love, so that you don't need another.

Now look at this passage:

"For the commandment is a lamp, And the law a light; Reproofs of instruction are the way of life, To keep you from the evil woman, From the flattering tongue of a seductress. Do not lust after her beauty in your heart, Nor let her allure you with her eyelids. For by means of a harlot A man is reduced to a <u>crust of bread</u>; And an adulteress will prey upon his precious life."

Proverbs 6:23-26 NKJV

Again we see financial destruction as the man is brought to a **crust of bread**. Read on:

"Can a man take fire to his bosom, And his clothes not be burned? Can one walk on hot coals, And his feet not be seared? So is he who goes in to his neighbor's wife; Whoever touches her shall not be innocent. People do not despise a thief If he steals to satisfy himself when he is starving. Yet when he is found, he must restore sevenfold;

He may have to give up <u>all the substance of his house</u>. Whoever commits adultery with a woman lacks understanding; He who does so <u>destroys his own soul</u>. <u>Wounds and dishonor</u> he will get, And his <u>reproach</u> will not be wiped away. For jealousy is a husband's fury; Therefore he will not spare in the day of vengeance. He will accept no recompense, Nor will he be appeased though you give many gifts."

Proverbs 6:27-35 NKJV

Wow! "But you say I've never touched anyone's wife." Jesus said looking to lust is just the same, which means spiritually it will open the same doors. Look at the consequences:

1. All the substance of your house

2. **Destruction of your own soul**
3. **Wounding and dishonor**
4. **Reproach**

Again and again we see that sexual sin will result in financial loss and struggle, not to mention emptiness to the soul and loss of honor. You have but to look at the news to see as both pastors and politicians have fallen into this trap, right along with average men who end up in a sting operation because they have contacted someone online, not knowing they are a police officer.

NATIONAL REPENTANCE

Is it not possible that our own national financial climate is somewhat affected by this wholesale rejection of God's moral code? Or does the phrase "God bless America" really mean anything? Can He continue to bless us when we defiantly betray His instructions? I would love to see what would happen if America would repent to the Lord for such abusive treatment of our sexuality, and see if He won't open up the windows of heaven in blessing over us!

Perhaps the crime that is gripping our neighborhoods would subside until it would be safe for our children to once again walk the streets, without fear that a rapist hyped up on several hours of unfulfilled sexual stimulation would strike and steal their innocence, and possibly their lives. And perhaps our wives would be safe at the local mall or grocery store parking lots without having to trust in a can of mace, that may or may not set them free from the grasp of their would be attacker.

Is the answer just to carry bigger guns? No! The real answer is slaying the dragon of pornography and its dreaded influence upon society; the real answer is men's hearts being changed by the delivering power of a forgiving God, who can cleanse their conscience and make new the heart. The *real* answer is Jesus!

I CAN CONTROL IT

Let's look at one more passage about the adulteress:

> *"Let not thine heart decline to her ways, go not astray in her paths. For she hath cast down many wounded: yea, many strong men have been slain by her. Her house is the way to hell, going down to the chambers of death."*
>
> *Proverbs 7:25-27 KJV*

Many *STRONG* men have been slain by her. Don't lie to yourself. If you are struggling, get help! Be honest with your wife and ask her to forgive you and help you escape this trap. RUN from it!

The good news is that there is forgiveness and deliverance for you. All sin may have a natural expression, but the root is a spiritual problem. Therapists can treat the mental response of the addiction, but true freedom comes from the restoration that only God can bring. Many seek to discount the spiritual realm simply because it cannot be graphed or measured, but there is a supernatural realm, and demonic forces do seek to enslave mankind through our human weaknesses. Jesus himself cast out the legion of demons that tormented the madman of Gadara in Mark 5:

> *"Then they came to the other side of the sea, to the country of the Gadarenes. And when He had come out of the boat, immediately there met Him out of the tombs a man with an unclean spirit, who had his dwelling among the tombs; and no one could bind*

him, not even with chains, because he had often been bound with shackles and chains. And the chains had been pulled apart by him, and the shackles broken in pieces; neither could anyone tame him. And always, night and day, he was in the mountains and in the tombs, crying out and cutting himself with stones. When he saw Jesus from afar, he ran and worshiped Him. And he cried out with a loud voice and said, 'What have I to do with You, Jesus, Son of the Most High God? I implore You by God that You do not torment me.' For He said to him, 'Come out of the man, unclean spirit!' Then He asked him, 'What is your name?' And he answered, saying, 'My name is Legion; for we are many...' Then they came to Jesus, and saw the one who had been demon-possessed and had the legion, sitting and clothed and in his right mind...And when He got into the boat, he who had been demon-possessed begged Him that he might be with Him. However, Jesus did not permit him, but said to him, 'Go home to your friends, and tell them what great things the Lord has done for you, and how He has had compassion on you.'"

Mark 5:1-9,15a, 18-19 NKJV

Jesus is still the Savior and Deliverer today, and will set free anyone who will come to Him in sincerity and truth. He has given this authority to His believers as well:

"And He said to them, 'Go into all the world and preach the gospel to every creature. He who believes and is baptized will be saved; but he who does not believe will be condemned. And these signs will follow those who believe: In My name they will cast out demons...'"

Mark 16:15-17a NKJV

You can be free and be restored again! You can slay the dragon of sexual addiction! Ask God to forgive you and to set you free. Turn away from sin (disobeying God's laws) and ask Jesus to be your Savior. Then find a good spirit-filled church that believes in God's power to deliver, and ask for help. There are also ministries that specialize in ministering to those with sexual addiction, but make sure they address the spiritual bondage as well as the psychological aspects of addiction. Counseling alone may bring a remedy, but Jesus is the cure!

He said it this way:

> *"...If you abide in My word, you are My disciples indeed. And you shall know* (experience) *the truth, and the truth shall make you free."*
> *John 8:31b-32 NKJV*

And:

> *"Therefore if the Son makes you free, you shall be free indeed."*
> *John 8:36 NKJV*

CHAPTER 11

HELPFUL HINTS FOR A HAPPY WIFE

Some men don't believe it's possible to please a woman. Then again, some men just aren't up to the task. There is a humorous story that was passed along to me some time ago that I would like to share.

A store in New York has just opened up where a woman may go to choose a husband. At the store's entrance is a list of instructions as to how the store operates:

1. You may visit this store only once.
2. There are six floors and the value of the product increases as you ascend.
3. You may either choose any item from the floor, or choose to go up to the next floor.
4. You cannot go back down to any previous floor except to exit the building.
5. Thank you for shopping at the Husband Store.

So a woman goes to the Husband Store and on the first floor she finds a sign on the door that reads, "Floor 1: These men have jobs."

She then proceeds to the second floor and the sign reads, "Floor 2: These men have jobs and love kids."

So she continues to the third floor and the sign on the door reads, "Floor 3: These men have jobs, love kids, and are extremely good-looking." "My," she exclaims and keeps ascending.

At the fourth floor, she finds a sign that says, "Floor 4: These men have jobs, love kids, are extremely good-looking, and help with the housework."

"Mercy me," she says. "I can hardly stand it!" and she continues upward. The fifth floor sign reads, "Floor 5: These men have jobs, love kids, are extremely good-looking, help with the housework, and have a strong romantic streak."

She is very tempted to stay, but still chooses to go on to the sixth floor. When she arrives, she finds a sign that reads:

"Floor 6: You are visitor number 31,456,012 to this floor. There are no men on this floor. This floor exists solely to prove that women are impossible to please! Thank you for shopping at the Husband Store."

You may have felt like that before, but hopefully now you have gained some understanding and insight in how to understand, value, and please your wife.

My wife handed me a "grass catcher" list when I went off to write this book. On it she listed some of the things she has dealt with as she has counseled women, and I think it would benefit us greatly to take this list to heart. I will give them to you just as she gave them to me:

1. Be a gentleman and treat your wife good.
2. Use soap and cologne before making love; scents turn a woman on or off. And wear something attractive; this shows you are putting some effort into lovemaking.
3. Don't expect your wife to lose weight and look good if you look nine months pregnant.
4. Help your wife, especially if she has young children, to put them to bed so she is not working until 9 or 10 at night, and then is expected to come in refreshed to make love.
5. Don't make a wife have to nag you to get things done around the house. Have motivation and don't watch TV all the time. Limit yourself and keep up with responsibilities.
6. Do acts of kindness to show your wife love.
7. Discipline the kids and don't allow them to ever talk back to their mother. Back your wife up and discuss disagreements about the kids in private. Do not allow kids to play one against the other. If your wife is a nag, it might be showing *your* lack of leadership.
8. If your wife works outside the home, then share the responsibilities of the home and get the kids also involved in the chores.
9. Tell your wife she's beautiful; leave her love notes. Don't say I told you I loved you twenty years ago. What if she said, we had sex twenty years ago...

These are directly from her handwritten paper, and are some of the things wives are saying that would make them happy. Remember the saying, "Happy wife, happy life!"

You know what, when you really love your wife these things are a joy. So I want you to do something for me. Ask your wife to make a list of the things she thinks "other women" might want their husbands to know; things that would make them happy. Then take the list and see if you have any area that could stand improvement.

CHAPTER 12

REJOICE WITH THE WIFE OF YOUR YOUTH!

M arriage is a gift from God and He wants you to **rejoice with your wife**!

"Let your fountain be blessed, and <u>rejoice with the wife of your youth</u>."

Proverbs 5:18 NKJV

That means you are supposed to be like newlyweds all the days of your life. God wants you happy and blessed in every way. You are God's power couple, blessed by Him to have dominion together in life. When you value the gifts in your wife, God will bless you, and together you will reign as God's king and queen! You will have a sound base for your home, and stability for your children. Yes, he who loves his wife loves himself!

We have looked at many ways that we can understand, value, and love our wives. What an absolute treasure from God your wife is. When God created the earth, He called everything good, but when He made man and woman, He said it was *very* good! You are the height of God's creative process, and the Bible says that the man who **finds a wife, finds a good thing**!!

> *"He who finds a wife finds a good thing, and obtains favor from the LORD."*
> *Proverbs 18:22 NKJV*

Just as sexual sins brings a curse, your marriage covenant brings the blessing of the Lord. Your wife is your **favor**! Favor is God's force to draw blessing to your life!

Let's close with three things that can keep that favor flowing.

CHERISH YOUR WIFE

Ephesians tells us to **cherish** her:

> *"So husbands ought to love their own wives as their own bodies; he who loves his wife loves himself. For no one ever hated his own flesh, but nourishes and cherishes it, just as the Lord does the church."*
> *Ephesians 5:28-29 NKJV*

Nourish means to "pamper." Men, forget queen for a day. How about queen for life! Make sure you pamper your wife by making sure she gets time for herself. Go out of your way to do things special for her. If you treat her like a queen, she'll end up treating you like a king!

Cherish means to brood over, or literally, "make a fuss" over her. She is special, and should always feel that way. Go out of your way to open doors for her, pull out her chair for her, and especially in public, make sure she is honored in the eyes of others (and not just to make yourself look good). What's done in public will find its way into your private life.

Love her as your own body! We take good care of ourselves. We feed ourselves when we are hungry, have our favorite chair at home, and so on. He who loves his wife loves himself. When you meet her needs, she'll meet yours.

VALUE YOUR WIFE

What you honor you keep, but what you take for granted you lose. We want our wives to respect us, but we are also supposed to honor them too.

> *"Likewise, ye husbands, dwell with them according to knowledge, giving <u>honor</u> unto the wife, as unto the weaker vessel, and as being heirs together of the grace of life: that your prayers be not hindered."*
> *I Peter 3:7 KJV*

We touched on this earlier in the book, but it is a key principle. This word for **honor** in the Greek means "value or money paid." You are not only to value your wife, but also make sure she has mall money! When you take care of your wife financially, it makes her feel valued. It is very important for a woman, and will reflect back on you. You are heirs together; remember the nuclear keys? Without her, the power isn't released, so make sure you honor her with words, deeds, and finances too.

PRAISE YOUR WIFE!

You should literally shower your wife with praise. It's part of washing her with your words. It brings to her a sense of worth, and causes her to want to live up to your words. Words are like the rudder of a ship, steering our lives. Don't leave your wife in dry dock! Flood her with words, and follow up with actions.

> *"Her children arise and call her blessed; her husband also, and he praises her."*
>
> *Proverbs 31:28 NIV*

Have you showered your wife with praise lately? There's no time like the present!

So what are you waiting for? Hey man, *Love your Woman*!

CHAPTER 13

GOD'S PROMISE FOR YOU

Though we may never have the opportunity to meet, I believe God has spoken to you through these pages. I encourage you to take the time right now to pray this prayer out loud over your life.

"Dear God,

I know that I am a sinner and I ask you to forgive me. I believe that Jesus died on the cross to pay for my sins and rose again to defeat the power of death. I receive your full pardon and declare Jesus Christ to be the Lord of my life. I commit to live a life that honors You and to lead my home as a godly man. I receive Your free gift of eternal life and Your power to live in victory every day. I believe that I am now a new man, and I pray these things in the Name of Jesus, Amen."

Congratulations, if you prayed that prayer in sincerity, you are now a part of the family of God. Make a fresh commitment today to find a good spirit-filled church where you can grow as a Christian and find other men to encourage you in your walk with God. Talk to Him daily and read His Word to find out all of His plans and promises for you.

ENDNOTES

(1) *Victory in Jesus*; words and music by E.M. Bartlett © 1939. Administrated by Integrated Copyright Group, Inc. All rights reserved.

(2) *His Needs, Her Needs* by Willard F. Harley Jr. Publisher: Revell; (April 1, 2001)

(3) http://www.womanspassions.com/articles/570.html; retrieved 12/19/10h

(4) *Men Are from Mars, Women Are from Venus: The Classic Guide to Understanding the Opposite Sex* by John Gray (Jan 6, 2004) Publisher: Harper Paperbacks

(5) http://www.womanspassions.com/articles/570.html; retrieved 12/2/10

(6) http://www.mastersofhealthcare.com/blog/2009/10-big-differences-between-mens-and-womens-brains/ By Amber Hensley, 6/16/09, retrieved 12/2/10

(7) http://www.power-surge.com/educate/menoprimer. htm; retrieved 12/2/10

(8) *Barriers to Communication: Hurt. Anger, and Fear* by Dr. Gary Chapman; Marriage Focus 6/16/10 http://www.marragevine.com

(9) Strong's Concordance, GR5093 James Strong; Hendrickson Publishers; Updated edition (June 30, 2007)

(10) http://advice.eharmony.com/article/fact-or-myth-is-chocolate-an-aphrodisiac.html by Steve Carter, Ph.D. retrieved 12/2/10

(11) http://www.ehouw.com/about_534397_Sensitive_parts_body.html; retrieved 12/7/10

(12) *Slow Hand*, written by John Bettis & James Bruce Clark, recorded by the Pointer Sisters, Black and White album, 1981

(13) http://dictionary.reference.com/browse/pornography retrieved 12/2/10

(14) http://www.healthboards.com/boards/showthread.php?t=581650 Can porn desensitize? Retrieved 12/7/10

(15) http://answers.yahoo.com/question/index?qid=200 80531234527AAk6Aqu Desensitized by Porn? How long to Resensitize? Retrieved 12/7/10

(16) Gene McConnell and Keith Campbell, *Dare to Dig Deeper* booklet "Toxic Porn" Copyright ©1996 Focus on the Family.

(17) http://www.medhelp.org/posts/Mens-Health/22-with-porn-induced-erectile-dysfunction/show/469209 Retrieved 12/8/10

ABOUT US

Douglas Michael Bankson is an author, pastor, teacher, singer/songwriter, and musician, who has been in full time ministry nationally and internationally for over 27 years. He and his wife Jeri are founding senior pastors of Victory Church World Outreach Center in Apopka, Florida. Together they minister the Word and Spirit of God, and have a special ministry and desire to see marriages strengthened and filled with passion.

Pastors Doug and Jeri Bankson have four wonderful and talented children, Benjamin, Joseph, Michael, and Victoria. All of their children are actively involved in the ministry, preaching, teaching and leading in praise and worship.

Also available:

For booking information or to order *Love Your Woman* or *Love Your Man*, contact:

Victory Church World Outreach Center
509 S Park Avenue, Apopka, FL 32703
407.889.7288
www.victorychurch.cc

LaVergne, TN USA
26 January 2011
214040LV00002B/2/P